CLOSE-UP MAGIC SECRETS

DIAMOND JIM TYLER

PHOTOGRAPHS BY JIM AND KATHY TYLER
EDITED BY ROBERT ZAFRAN AND DR. SUE COFFMAN
INTRODUCTION BY JEFF DAVIS
FOREWORD BY JON RACHERBAUMER

DOVER PUBLICATIONS, INC.
MINEOLA, NEW YORK

Bibliographical Note

This Dover edition, first published in 2011, is a slightly corrected republication of the work originally published by Diamond Jim Productions, Irving, Texas, in 2000 under the title and subtitle *Pockets Full of Miracles: Secrets from the Repertoire of a Professional Close-Up Magician.*

Library of Congress Cataloging-in-Publication Data

Tyler, Diamond Jim.
    Close-up magic secrets / Diamond Jim Tyler ; photographs by Jim and Kathy Tyler ; edited by Robert Zafran and Dr. Sue Coffman ; introduction by Jeff Davis ; foreword by Jon Racherbaumer.
        p. cm.
    Summary: "A professional performer presents tricks for magicians at every level of skill, especially novices. Intended for performances in bars, restaurants, and other close-up venues, these 29 routines include original tricks as well as tried-and-true crowd pleasers. Over 300 photographs illustrate clear instructions for illusions involving cards, money, fire, mind reading, and comedy"—Provided by publisher.
    ISBN-13: 978-0-486-47891-3 (pbk.)
    ISBN-10: 0-486-47891-2 (pbk.)
    1. Magic tricks. I. Zafran, Robert. II. Coffman, Sue. III. Tyler, Diamond Jim. Pockets full of miracles. IV. Title.

GV1547.T94 2011
793.8—dc22

                                                    2010048666

Manufactured in the United States by Courier Corporation
47891201
www.doverpublications.com

Close-Up Magic Secrets

by Diamond Jim Tyler

♦

Photographs by
Jim and Kathy Tyler

♣

Edited by
Robert Zafran and Dr. Sue Coffman

♥

Introduction by
Jeff Davis

♠

Foreword by
Jon Racherbaumer

Dedicated to the memory of

Lewis Zafran

1915 – 1997

In a galaxy full of magic,
Lew was a comet which shone so brightly
that all who watched as he passed,
stood in awe!

CONTENTS

Introduction by Jeff Davis
Foreword by Jon Racherbaumer
A Night in the Life of Diamond Jim

INTRODUCTION
by Jeff Davis

Many magicians have escaped or "cheated" death. But isn't it always a trick? Diamond Jim Tyler once performed a feat that even the great Houdini himself never equaled.

Jim is somewhat of an enigma. He has a wicked sense of humor that belies his polite demeanor. I first laid eyes on Jim in 1986. He was honing his skills as a magician the same way I had done it more than ten years earlier, by working and demonstrating magic at a local magic shop. A terrarium on the counter contained a fake tarantula. Or so I thought. If you've never seen a tarantula up close, it often remains motionless for such long periods that you'd swear it's a fake.

I was staring at the tarantula trying to determine whether it was indeed real or just a joke. My face was just inches from the glass. Suddenly *another* tarantula jumped from *behind* the terrarium onto the counter! My heart skipped a beat. Jim laughed. I looked down at the counter and saw an obviously fake plastic spider with a hose attached. The other end of the hose was in Jim's hand. A squeeze from his hand had made the plastic spider jump at just the right time while the beast in the terrarium had misdirected my attention. But Jim's chuckle was about to turn into a belly laugh.

Convinced that the tarantula in the terrarium was also a fake and the danger was over, I again placed my face just inches from the glass. "But this one looks so real," I remarked, trying to look unrattled. "It is real," Jim insisted, but with a crooked smile.

"C'mon, you're not going to fool me again. If it's real, then why won't it move?" I challenged. My face was still inches from the glass, and I was now tapping on the side furiously. Suddenly, as if Jim somehow had the ability to control this living, breathing creature, the tarantula instantly jumped onto the glass RIGHT IN MY FACE! It was instantaneous, like a magic trick. Jim howled.

Lew Zafran, the man to whom this book is dedicated, was my great-uncle. Lew was a master at making friends. When I chose the pallbearers for Lew's funeral, I selected some of his oldest friends as well as some of his newest, including Jim Tyler. This was appropriate because Lew continued making new friends right up until his death. "I'd make friends with people my own age," he'd joke, "but there aren't any."

Among the most distraught at Lew's death was Jim Tyler, nearly sixty years his junior! "I've lost my best friend," he told me, echoing my sentiments. I've had the good fortune to get to know Jim a little better since then. I've seen him perform, had dinner with Jim and his wife, Kathy, and been a guest in their home. I've come to understand what Lew saw in Jim. He is energetic, enthusiastic, and dedicated to being the best magician he can be. More important, he is a fine and decent person.

I'm happy that Lew inspired Jim to write this book, and I know Lew would be very proud. Many of the effects in this book are strong magic. Some might be dismissed as merely "cute" items. *Do not underestimate these items.* Lew knew, and Jim has learned, that these items can elevate a show from being ordinary to being truly *entertaining*. Items or effects such as these will endear you to your audiences.

Jim's goal was to write a book that would appeal to and benefit beginners as well as experienced magicians. He has succeeded. He has included a glossary for beginners, who often get frustrated by references to sleights that are unfamiliar to them. (Check the glossary if you don't know what a sleight is!) Many of the tricks, such as Burning Impression and The Birthday Bill, require very little sleight-of-hand and are easy to do. Yet they get terrific response from an audience. For the more experienced finger-flingers, check out One-Armed Aces, Trapdoor Coins, and Diamond's Dazzler. These knuckle-busters should keep you busy. Don't overlook some of the simpler items, such as Three Burnt Matches, Invisible Thumbscrews, and The Hitchhiker. With a little showmanship and the right personality, you can really have fun with these. As a bonus beyond the abundance of material, the book is also a fun read. Jim includes quotations from various sources that are amusing and sometimes thought-provoking. And his own sense of humor runs throughout.

So what has Jim done that Houdini failed to do? Of all Jim's accomplishments in life, his greatest feat is one that none of us would ever even hope to *attempt*. Jim beat cancer. I'm happy to report that he recently celebrated five years of his cancer being in remission. The medical experts say that means he is officially cured of Hodgkin's disease. And he really did celebrate. Had a pool party. I can't think of anything more worthy of a celebration. And his victory against cancer is good news for you. Otherwise, you wouldn't be holding this book in your hands. Celebrate and enjoy.

FOREWORD
by Jon Racherbaumer

Diamond Jim Tyler, to echo Mike Close's useful cognomen, is a *worker*. That is, he has spent many years plying and perfecting his trade *with* laypeople, not just other magicians. And he did so in the challenging environment we call the *real world*, doing it under fire in real-life conditions. This makes a big difference, and this is a difference you will discover as you study this compressed field manual of Tyler's *personal* research and development.

Close-Up Magic Secrets contains *29 presentations* (not tricks) which have a proven track record. They have been tried, tested and confirmed by Tyler over many years, with many kinds of audiences. They work. They "get the money." They are, to use Close's other definition of the term, "workers." In other words, they fall under an enduring category (of trick) where "every last performance detail has been thought out," including all patter, misdirection, and audience management—not to mention the actual action steps of the physical presentation.

Back in the 1970s, when close-up magic began grabbing the attention of amateur magicians in a big way, restaurant magic was the venue of the day, also leading to the atmospheric, episodic venue now called walk-around or strolling magic. Prior to this, there were only a few well-known restaurant-bar magicians: Bert Allerton, Dr. Jaks, Matt Schulien, Johnny Paul, Jim Ryan, Hebe Haba Al and Don Alan. When this trend gained momentum, I was asked by a renowned restaurant owner in New Orleans to perform at one of his establishments, a place called P.O.E.T.S.. I worked there for about three years, and it proved to be an enlightening experience. At the time I knew lots of tricks and hundreds of others were readily available. There was no shortage of apparently good material. So when I began, my three close-up cases were jam-packed with the latest "stuff." My pockets bulged with packet tricks, sponge balls, color-changing knives, chop cups, invisible thread—you name it! I also had dozens of "magician-foolers" in my rehearsed repertoire; I was ready to knock them dead. However, what I quickly learned was the truth of Eugene Burger's observation that "professional magicians perform the same tricks for different spectators, whereas amateur magicians perform different tricks for the *same* spectators." Although I had lots of different tricks, many audience-tested on magicians, I did not have a repertoire of "workers." After six weeks of trial-and-error, hitting and missing, and undergoing a barrage of reality checks, I dumped most of the stuff in my close-up cases and slowly started discovering what worked and didn't work. It took three months to develop about six "workers."

I mention my own experience along these lines because at the time there were a small number of guidebooks regarding this venue. Mike Close, Eugene Burger and others had not yet written their books. Today, aspiring magicians are lucky. There are many books written by "workers" who "have been there, done that". Take advantage of them. Take advantage of Diamond Jim Tyler's experience. His book, the one now in your hands, is a distillation of his hard-earned experience working in the trenches. It is his testament and gift to you. If you like, perform each presentation as it is written. Play around. Test. Enjoy the helpful glossary. However, I suggest that you study the underlying approaches afterward and examine what is sometimes called *subtext*. If you do this, reading between the lines as well, you will be rewarded. You will save yourself a lot of time and trouble, expediting your own progress on the hardscrabble road to becoming a "worker." It worked for Diamond Jim. It can work for you.

January 1, 2000
New Orleans, Louisiana

A Night in the Life of Diamond Jim

I've arrived at my destination and anticipate all of the individuals that I'm soon to meet. As I throw on my jacket, I look up at the night sky and take in a deep breath. Exhaling a sigh of happiness, I enter the place, welcomed by handshakes and the call of my name. Life is good and my pockets are full of miracles.

Whose life should I brighten first? Should I go to young Taylor, who brings his parents each week to see me? Or should I enter the bar, where three of the regulars are waving me to come over? Hoping I've made the right choice, I go into the bar and tell my three friends, "I'll be back shortly." They smile and promise to wait until I can make it back.

Taylor and his parents act impressed and once again treat me as if I'm a celebrity. My three pals in the bar plead with me to show them a trick I know they've seen at least a dozen times. I comply with the request of my three friends, but only after showing them something new. Magically the evening seems to fly by as I respond to each request.

As I drive back home, I think back on the night and reminisce about each smile, laugh, scream and look of amazement. I've visited with some old friends. I've made some new friends. The next time any of these friends comes to a crossroads in life or feels that they've come up against something that is impossible, hopefully they'll remember my magic and realize that when people change their perception of things, they can change the world!

What you will soon read has served me well, placing bread in my pocket as well as on the table. *Close-Up Magic Secrets* is filled with many of my own routines as well as my adaptations of effects that I feel are worth performing.

My repertoire, like my life, is filled with variety. Within these covers you will find routines involving cards, money, fire, gags, bar-betchas, mind-reading, comedy and more.

In the school of magic, I have no idea at what level, or in what category, you would place yourself. With that in mind, I have tried to create a book for every type of magician. With the descriptive text and numerous photos I have tried to capture every nuance during each routine. In addition, each term that falls into the category of "magic jargon" has been bold-faced. These bold-faced words are defined in the glossary at the back of the book.

I have also tried to give credit where credit is due. If I have neglected anyone, magician or otherwise, please notify me so that changes can be made to later editions. My late friend Lew Zafran was the inspiration for putting my thoughts on paper. Some of the routines you'll read were his own or were done with his collaboration.

Please do not read this book as if it were an instruction manual for simple tricks. Take the time to read between the lines, and I promise that you will find some of the true secrets of magic. A successful magician is not measured by the quantity of effects he or she learns. The important thing, as in most professions, is the quality of what you know. So be prepared. . . .

You're about to learn how to do some incredible mind-blowing magic!

Magically yours,

Diamond Jim Tyler

◆ ◆ ◆

The Gunslinger

"When things look bad, and it looks like you're not gonna make it, you gotta get mean. I mean plumb mad dog mean, because if you lose your head, and you give up, then you neither live nor win; that's just the way it is." - Clint Eastwood in *The Outlaw Josey Wales*

Effect: A black Jack is selected, referred to as Cowboy Jack, and signed across the face by a spectator. The magician proceeds to create a Wild West scenario by drawing a cowboy-gunslinger stick figure on the back of the chosen card. The card cowboy is placed upright on a table, a few feet away from the magician. The magician challenges the card cowboy to a gunfight! A few seconds later the magician pulls out an imaginary gun, and POW! The cowboy falls over dead!

The magician hands the card to the spectator to reveal the fresh bullet hole in the card. Upon examining the card, the magician comments that it looks as if the bullet missed the stick figure. Yet when the card is turned face up, it is revealed that the bullet has actually penetrated the heart of the Jack. WOW!

Required Items:
♦ A hole-puncher
♦ A black Sharpie® indelible marker
♦ A bunch of black Jacks, if you plan to repeat the effect
♦ A red-back deck of good-quality cards with a busy back design.
  I prefer Poker Bicycle® cards.

Figure 1

Preparation: Looking at the face of the black Jack, punch a hole in the card where the Jack's heart should be (FIG.1). Remove the punch-out from the hole-puncher and place it back into the card so that it appears whole again. Working on a flat surface, and following the pattern of the card, align the punch-out properly, and press it flush into place. Rub the gaffed or prepared area in a circular motion with the back of your fingernail. Once this is done, place the gaffed Jack into the deck at the position that you wish to force it. *For this effect, I choose to place the Jack on the face of the deck so that I may execute the **Hindu Shuffle Force**.*

The Vortex Move: Basically, as if by magic, the move knocks over a card that has been stood upright several feet from the magician. In short, you use a backhand motion. As you approach the tabletop, your hand should stop suddenly and point at the card, and it will fall over a second later.

The move works by creating a vortex of air along the tabletop. The position of your hand will send the vortex in the direction of the card (FIG. 2). Amazingly, your hand appears to be far away, and perfectly still, when the card falls over. Practice the move by placing the card farther away each time you try it. Obviously, it would be beneficial for you to know exactly how close the card must be for the move to work every time.

Figure 2

The following section explains how to make such an unnatural movement seem natural.

Executing the Vortex Move: To begin, bend a playing card lengthwise from edge to edge, putting a natural bow in the card. Do not crease the card (FIG. 3). Place the card vertically a few feet away on a nearby counter or tabletop. Make sure there is a clear path between you and the card. Stand near the edge of the table, which should be about waist level, and place your hands naturally at your side. Prepare yourself for the Vortex Move.

Figure 3

To execute the move, use your right hand, pretending to draw an imaginary gun from your left side. Keep the fingers of your right hand straight, and swiftly move your right hand toward the tabletop. Stop suddenly several feet away, once your hand is in perfect alignment with the card (FIG. 2). Quickly, make a gun with your right hand and pretend to shoot the card. Once the card begins to topple over, mimic the action of the gun recoiling with your right hand. Afterward, pretend to blow away the smoke from the barrel of the gun; this subtlety brings your hand closer to you, emphasizing the magic.

This move is an essential part of the effect, so practice it over and over again until you can do it every time. Make sure you do not touch the tabletop. You don't want anyone thinking you jarred it. Also emphasize the fact that your hand is several feet from the card when the magic happens. You will know you have the move perfected when the card seems to fall over seconds later, after your hand has ceased its motion.

Routine: After forcing the Jack, place it on a flat surface and ask the spectator to sign it across the face. Do not worry about him or her signing across the gaffed area; it will stay intact. Begin your story of how fast you have to be with your hands to be a magician. Explain that had you been born in the Wild West days, you might have chosen to be a gunslinger, using your special talent to defend your town's honor.

Perpetuating the mood, create the bad guy, Cowboy Jack. Draw an ornery-looking cowboy on the back of the selected card. Be careful not to draw on top of the gaffed area; later it should appear as if the bullet has missed Cowboy Jack (FIG. 4).

Figure 4

Hold the card face down and proceed to bend the card lengthwise, back edge to back edge. Make just a slight bow in the card, enough to make it stand up. Use your left hand's thumb and index finger to pinch the front and back of the gaffed area. Use the other hand to help bend it, with the same grip, so the hole will not accidentally pop out (FIG. 3). Stand the card vertically a few feet from where you are standing.

Speak of the showdown about to take place as you face your opponent eye to eye. Prepare Cowboy Jack, and the audience, by stating that you will draw on the count of three. After the count, suddenly go for your imaginary gun and execute the Vortex Move. Say "Pow!" as the card starts to fall over. The count of "1, 2, 3" and saying "Pow!" help assure that you did not blow Cowboy Jack over with your breath.

Once the card has fallen, your audience will be amazed. During this moment, pick up the tabled face-down card with your right hand, not calling any attention to it. Approach the card with your left hand and place your thumbnail on top of the gaffed area, and your index finger beneath it. Push the punch-out onto your waiting index finger with the thumbnail of your left hand. Using your right hand, slide the card into a position where you are pinching not only the uppermost portion of the card, but the concealed punch-out as well.

Finally, call attention to the newly formed hole in the back of the card. Show the audience that it seems you were a bad shot and missed the stick-figure cowboy completely. Let this idea sink in, then turn over the card to reveal, to everyone's surprise, that actually the heart of the bad guy Cowboy Jack has been penetrated. Hand the spectator the signed selection as evidence, and to keep as a souvenir, while slipping the punch-out away with your index finger and thumb. Inconspicuously, let your left hand fall to your side to drop the punch-out onto the floor, or place it in your pocket as you put away the cards or the Sharpie® marker.

If you would like to add a sound effect to the imaginary gun, visit your local novelty store. There you will find an item called a bingo device. This small device makes a loud bang using a small round cap. You could hide the device in your hand or in your jacket. The bingo device can be quite loud, so practice common sense when using it.

As far as I know, Michael Weber fathered the idea of punching out a hole and replacing it. This novel idea appears in his book Life Savers *under the heading of "The One-Two Punch". The routine centers on the idea of moving a hole from one ticket and placing it in another. Buy the book and you'll discover a cornucopia of close-up miracles.*

New Age Spellbound

"The eye altering, alters all."
William Blake
The Mental Traveler

<u>Effect</u>: A glass stone magically changes colors repeatedly.

This is the classic **Spellbound** routine, done with glass stones and with an alternate handling. Making an American silver half-dollar change to an English copper penny has always been an amazing feat. Watching a coin change its metal content rather than changing the coin's nationality bewilders the audience. Thus, with the following routine, I believe I have captured the essence of this effect during this era of crystal power.

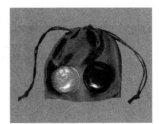

Figure 1

Required Items:

◆ Two stones of different colors, made of stained glass (FIG. 1). *The stones can be found at any good art-supply store. The stones are usually about the size of an American half-dollar. I prefer that one of the stones be clear and the other black. Each stone is unique in that one side is rounded and the other side is flat. The stones are not perfectly circular, so try to match two that are similar.*

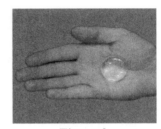

Figure 2

◆ A small drawstring bag to hold one of the stones (FIG. 1). *I like to visit occult shops to find the bags. The bag will act as cover near the end of the routine. The bag also adds to the mystique of the effect.*

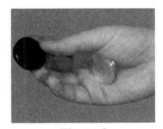

Figure 3

The Routine:

I. First Change (Cover Switch)

Start with the black stone in the bag and the clear stone **Classic Palmed** (FIG. 2) in your right hand, with the flat side toward your palm. Open the bag with both hands and pour its contents onto the table, placing the bag nearby. Pick up the black stone with the tips of your right hand's fingers while placing your thumb on the back of the flat side (FIG. 3). Display the black stone by turning your hand upward to the spectators (FIG. 4). Do not expose the clear stone.

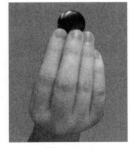

Figure 4

Raise your left arm about waist high and place the black stone into the **French Drop** position in your left hand (FIG. 5). Allow your right arm to relax at your side,

Figure 5

and let the palmed clear stone flip over into **Finger Grip** position, with the flat side facing saway from your fingertips (FIG. 6). Bring your right arm up, and allow your right hand, with closed fingers, to come past the black stone in your left hand (FIG. 7). Once no stones are visible to the audience, use your left thumb to pivot the black stone toward your right arm. Keep the right side of your body directed toward the audience to help cover the secret actions of your hands.

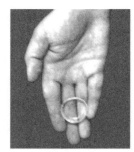

Figure 6

Grip the black stone in the **Thumb Palm** position with your right hand, as shown in FIG. 8, while placing the clear stone in its place. Watch your angles and your cover. Make sure the stones do not click, and then come away with your right hand, letting your right arm relax at your side. Once your right arm is relaxed, let the black stone fall into the Finger Grip position, with the flat side away from your fingertips.

Figure 7

II. Second Change (French Drop Switch)
Bring your right hand up in front, with the clear stone held at the fingertips of your left hand. Hold the black stone in the Finger Grip position, with your right thumb against the backside of the black stone. Push the clear stone into your left hand with the back of your right thumb, putting the black stone into its place (FIG. 9). Note that the clear stone should be resting on your left hand's fingers, not touching your palm, with the black stone in front of the clear stone.

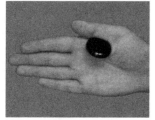

Figure 8

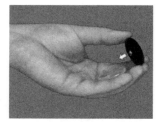

Figure 9

During the routine, remember always to keep the stone in your left hand directed toward the spectators' eyes to avoid any bad angles. As you bring your right hand away, gesture with an open hand, not saying a word. Actions speak louder than words at this point.

III. Third Change (Reverse French Drop)

As you bring your right hand up in front of your left hand, Thumb Palm the black stone with your right hand (FIG. 10). While your right hand is in front of your left hand, lower your left thumb to push and lift the clear stone back into the French Drop position. This should all be done in one action. As you do this, make sure your left hand does not bob up or down behind your blocking right hand. Let your right arm relax again and place the black stone into the Finger Grip position.

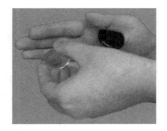

Figure 10

IV. Last Change (Jimbo Switch)

Note that in J. B. Bobo's *Modern Coin Magic*, the author reveals a magical coin exchange called the **Bobo Switch.** During this switch, the coin that will be exchanged with the original coin is placed in the **Finger Rest** position. The Jimbo Switch suggests that the coin or object that will be exchanged with the original object is placed in the Classic Palm position. This maneuver helps to prevent the risk of any clicking noise from the two glass stones. And it makes the guilty hand appear empty.

As your right hand comes up to grab the clear stone, Classic Palm the black stone. Next, toss the clear stone into your left hand, clenching it in a fist as you do so. Repeat this "take and toss" action again, making sure your hands remain somewhat close together. On the third toss, execute the Jimbo Switch (FIG. 11). As the switch is made, clench your left hand into a fist quickly, hiding the black stone from the audience's view. Let your right arm relax, with the clear stone in the Finger Grip position.

Figure 11

V. The Final Touch (Kaps' Subtlety)

Open your left hand and reveal the black stone to the audience. As your right hand approaches your left hand, Classic Palm the clear stone. Hold your right hand as

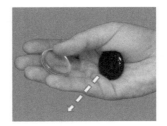

Figure 12

shown in FIG. 12 and grab the black stone. Your right hand's thumb should be touching the black stone while the fingers of your right hand rest against the back of your left hand. Slide the black stone out of your left hand onto your right hand's fingertips. The crotch of your right hand's thumb and the angle of your left hand will hide the clear stone from view; this is known as

Kap's Subtlety.

Turn your right hand palm down as you hand the black stone to a spectator for examination. At this point, let your right arm relax, allowing the clear stone to fall into Finger Grip position. Your right hand should approach the table to pick up the bag and place the clear stone on top of it. Turn your right hand and the bag over, hiding the clear stone between your fingers and the bag. Take back the black stone and place it in the bag (FIG. 13). Draw the strings of the bag closed. Place everything in your right hand in your pocket. Now the effect is immediately repeatable for the next group.

Figure 13

There are many maneuvers used to create this simple effect. Practice each one and perfect it. When performing New Age Spellbound, make sure your audience is directly in front of you. Keep eye contact with the audience or look where you wish them to look. If it makes you feel comfortable, tell a story while misdirecting their attention. Please do not overstate the obvious while they are watching. Practice in front of a mirror, not on your audience!

You will discover Dai Vernon's original handling of the Spellbound routine in one of the best books ever compiled on the art of close-up magic: Stars of Magic, *published by D. Robbins & Co., Inc.*

One-Armed Aces

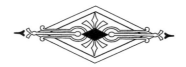

"I'd give my right arm to be ambidextrous."
Unknown

Effect: The magician performs a one-hand cut, and an Ace leaps face up onto the table. The audience is amazed. The magician successfully repeats this twice. Unfortunately, on his fourth and final attempt, the magician cuts to a Joker. The Joker is placed face down near the other three Aces. The magician exclaims, "Oh! I forgot. Jokers are wild." As he flips the Joker face up, it magically changes to the last Ace.

<u>Required Items</u>:
- ♦ A deck of good-quality cards
- ♦ Two convex **breather cards**

I prefer to use the Jokers as the breathers. The breather cards' impressions must be put into the back of the Jokers for this effect. The Jokers are the best two cards to remove from the pack, since they are not used in most card games or card magic. It's best to use a new deck for this effect.

Figure 1

<u>Preparation</u>: Have the Jokers (breathers) ready. Before stacking the deck, keep in mind that all of the cards will be face down in a face-down deck. Remove the four Aces from the deck. Place the two red Aces on top of the deck. Place one of the Jokers on the face of the deck (FIG. 1). Cut the deck near the middle, and complete the cut.

Place the Ace of Clubs on top of the deck. Then place the Ace of Spades on the face of the deck. Next, place the second Joker on the face of the deck, covering the Ace of Spades (FIG. 2). Finally, place the deck in the cardbox and you are ready to begin.

Figure 2

I have always loved card effects that involve finger-flinging or flourishes that demand the audience's respect. One-Armed Aces is my contribution to those who admire knuckle-busting sleight-of-hand card magic. I designed this effect around the flourish I reinvented: the Springboard Move, which makes the top card of the pack leap face up onto the table. This will take some practice to do every time, but it's worth the effort.

Figure 3

<u>How to execute the Springboard Move</u>:
Hold the deck face down in the **Dealer's Grip** (FIG. 3) with your left hand. With your left hand's thumb, push the top card of the deck toward and over your fingertips. Pivot the card with your fingertips and thumb, and position the card as shown in FIG. 4. The bottom left corner of the card should be touching the fleshy pad of your palm, just beneath your thumb.

Figure 4

With the tip of your middle finger, press on the top right corner of the card. Press inward until the card buckles upward and your middle finger is flush with the deck (FIG. 5). Simply pull the middle finger down while still pressing against the card, and it will leap from the deck. With some practice, you can cause the card to flip face up onto the table each time. Position your hand just above the tabletop so the leaping card has only a short distance to travel.

Perfect the Springboard Move before reading any further.

Figure 5

Routine: Remove the prearranged deck from its box. Give the deck a couple of **false shuffles** and/or **false cuts**. Explain that only the best cardmen can cut to an Ace. State that you can do it with only one hand. Take the deck in your left hand and execute the **Charlier Pass** (FIG. 6). As you do this, a Joker (breather card) should be cut to the face of the deck. This will place the two red Aces on top of the pack.

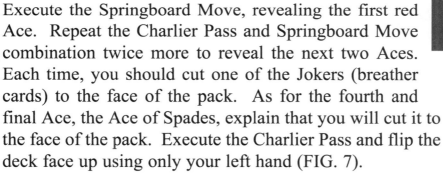

Figure 6

Execute the Springboard Move, revealing the first red Ace. Repeat the Charlier Pass and Springboard Move combination twice more to reveal the next two Aces. Each time, you should cut one of the Jokers (breather cards) to the face of the pack. As for the fourth and final Ace, the Ace of Spades, explain that you will cut it to the face of the pack. Execute the Charlier Pass and flip the deck face up using only your left hand (FIG. 7).

Figure 7

The audience will notice that you cut to a Joker. Say, "Oops! I can't believe I miscut, especially to a Joker, and this was supposed to be a serious card trick." The audience moans as you square the cards.

With your right hand, approach the Joker and execute a **double-lift**, concealing the Ace of Spades. With your right hand, place the **double** onto the deck while maintaining a **break** with your left hand's fingertips. Use your left hand's thumb to hold the double in place (FIG. 8). With your right hand, angle the double so the bottom right corner of the card

Figure 8

points outward, still using your left hand's thumb to hold it in place (FIG. 9).

Figure 9

Execute the **Down's Change**, placing the Ace of Spades face down near the other three face-up Aces. The audience should believe that the face-down card is a Joker. Place the deck on the table, being careful not to reveal the Joker on the face of the deck.

Act as if the light bulb in your head has just come on. Exclaim, "Oh! I forgot. Jokers are wild." As you say this, with your left hand's extended index finger, slowly and dramatically flip the face-down Ace of Spades face up on top of the other Aces (FIG. 10). The audience should be impressed.

Figure 10

When practicing this effect, you will discover that cutting to the breather cards may take some effort. If you find it difficult to cut a breather card each time, then it's probably best to make deeper impressions in the breathers. Remember, when you are performing the effect to peek at the card you are cutting to while executing the Charlier Pass, and if you notice the cut card is not a Joker, then square the pack and try again.

The inconsistency of using your right hand at the end of the effect is simply forgotten by most of the audience. Enacting the mistake of cutting to the wrong card overshadows the brief use of your right hand. You could learn, with much practice, to do the entire effect with one hand. But it's not necessary. Why run when no one is chasing you?

Since my book's first edition, I've learned that my Springboard Move is not completely unique with me. In 1983, Philippe Socrate of Paris, France published a similar move, called The Invisible Catapult *in his lecture notes. When practicing either of the moves or this effect, I suggest you try it with your eyes closed. Only when you can perform the One-Armed Aces without watching your hand do you truly have the effect mastered. So by all means, as the film* Star Wars *urged, "Use the force, Luke!"*

The Hitchhiker

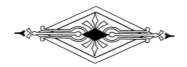

"Vision is the art of seeing things invisible."
Jonathan Swift
Thoughts on Various Subjects

<u>Effect</u>: The magician captures the audience's attention with a dollar bill, a vivid imagination and a bit of humor.

Sometimes it is fun to have a short interlude and converse with your audience while performing your magic. It is important to mingle with the crowd instead of always trying to amaze them. Take out a one-dollar bill or, better yet, borrow one. The following bit is an excellent way to lead into any one of your favorite dollar-bill tricks.

Figure 1

Begin by asking, "Does anyone know where the spider is on the face of a one-dollar bill?" Some will answer "Yes," and some will say "No." Permit the audience to search for a short while, and then show them where it is (FIGS. 1 & 2). *You may need a magnifying glass to show the audience.*

Figure 2

Then ask, "Does anyone know where the hitchhiker is on the back of a one-dollar bill?" *See if you can find the hitchhiker. He is next to the pyramid* (FIGS. 3 & 4).

Figure 3

After everyone has looked for a good while, to no avail, offer to show where he is. Take the bill and point next to the pyramid, saying, "See. He is right here." Bewildered, everyone will look closer. Finish by saying, "Oh! Wait a minute! Somebody must have picked him up!"

GOTCHA!

Figure 4

Obviously there is no magic involved here. However, there is a valuable lesson to be learned. Like any good effect, there is a surprise in the end. Try using this and other gags from time to time. It is important to have your audience like you. If they like you, they will more likely love your magic.

◆ ◆ ◆

Baseball Diamond

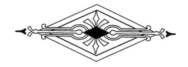

"Baseball is 90% mental, the other half is physical."
Yogi Berra

Effect: The spectator selects a baseball player whose picture appears on one card in a group of baseball cards. The magician explains that he will guess the name of the selection in three attempts. After a couple of failed attempts, the magician dumps a regulation baseball from within the cardbox, to everyone's surprise. Amazingly, the baseball is autographed by the player that the spectator chose.

Required Items:

◆ A large number of regular baseball cards and a cardbox. *I use a deck of playing cards with baseball players on them* (FIG. 1).

◆ A regulation baseball

◆ An ink pen

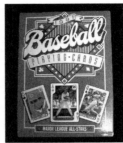

Figure 1

I've found it's best to wear a suit-jacket to hide the bulge from the baseball in your pants pocket during this routine.

Preparation: Choose the name of the baseball player that you prefer to force on your audience. Write, or have someone else write, in his or her best hand-writing, the name of the baseball player to be forced onto the ball. Place the signed baseball halfway into the top of your left pants pocket. Don't worry about the ball hanging out of your pants pocket. The ball will be covered by your suit-jacket. Place the baseball cards, in their box, somewhere on your person.

Presentation: Remove the cards from their box and show them to your audience. Explain to your audience, "As you can see, I have many Major League All-Stars to choose from. In just a moment I will have someone randomly select one of the players, and I will reveal his name in three attempts or less. If I get three strikes, then I'm out!" This effect should be presented as a bit of **mentalism** rather than a card trick.

Figure 2

Force your desired card on a spectator. *I prefer to use the* **Hindu Shuffle Force** *for this effect.* Let's say the card pictures *Rob Dibble*, for example (FIG. 2). Have the spectator show the card to the rest of the audience and hold on to it. If the spectator puts the card back in the deck, then your audience will assume that you are just doing another pick-a-card-and-watch-me-find-it trick. This effect demands more respect than that.

Make two failed guesses at revealing the card in order to build suspense. Your guesses could be close, since you know what the card is. As you scratch your head in thought with your right hand, allow your left hand to relax casually near your left pants pocket. Cup the baseball in your left hand as you say, "I made a prediction earlier today and placed it in the cardbox. Would you like to see what it says?" Upon the audience's response, use your right hand to place the cardbox on top of the baseball cupped in your left hand. The cardbox should be perpendicular to the table or floor while covering the baseball hidden in your hand.

Figure 3

Lift the flap of the cardbox with your right hand as you peek inside (FIG. 3). The top of the ball is covered by half of the cardbox. Watch the position of your left hand and your angles to avoid flashing the bottom of the ball. Say, "You're not gonna believe what my prediction says!" Turn the left hand down and pretend to dump the baseball from the cardbox.

Figure 4

Once the ball hits the table, your audience will jump. This is definitely a surprise. Before you start the routine, it is best to push up your sleeves for obvious reasons. The climax of the effect occurs when you reveal the autograph on the ball (FIG. 4). *After the fact, I usually act stupid and try to put the baseball back into the box, which reinforces the magic.*

The inspiration for this effect derives from the creative mind of John Bannon. Mr. Bannon published his effect entitled Trick Shot Production in his best-selling magic book Smoke and Mirrors. *Wanting to create something novel I envisioned Baseball Diamond after performing Bannon's "Eight Ball" version many times. You could just as easily make the effect your own by producing a different item from the cardbox.*

This routine makes a great opener. Productions have always been strong openers for any type of magic act. The award-winning magician Johnny Ace Palmer produces a bottle opener for his first effect. Johnny follows this by producing a bottle of Coke, which makes logical sense.

*This effect is an excellent example of how to turn on ordinary card trick into a fun bit of magic. Most people have probably seen an uncle **fan** through the pack to reveal a selected card. However, most people have probably never seen a baseball produced from thin air. Try not to make a move out of loading the baseball under the cardbox. Just do it. And, if this magic stuff doesn't pan out for you, then you could always make a living by forging autographed baseballs.*

The FBI Trick

"You asked for miracles; I give you the F. . . B. . . I."
Alan Rickman as Hans Gruber in *Die Hard*

Effect: A pair of thumbcuffs is introduced. After examining and wearing them, a volunteer locks the magician into the cuffs. Unbeknownst to the volunteer, the magician escapes from the cuffs time and again, causing a comical situation. After a few surprises, the thumbcuffs vanish right before the audience's eyes.

Thumbcuffs are a standard item sold in most magic or novelty stores. Although most magicians know what cuffs are and how to escape from them, few use them. The FBI Trick is one that can be performed while strolling through the audience or on a stage. Not only does this routine fit in a pocket and play for big crowds, but it could easily become one of your and your audiences' favorite comedy effects.

Required Items:
◆ A pair of thumbcuffs with keys (FIG. 1)
◆ A big swollen fake thumb (FIG. 2)
◆ A handkerchief

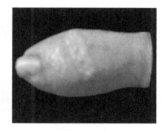
Figure 1

The fake thumb is sold in novelty stores and referred to as Horrible Finger; it usually sells for a couple of bucks. Remove the fake bloody bandage that is attached to the fake thumb. The thumb is made of thin latex and can be crumpled into a ball to be hidden in your hand. Place the handkerchief into your inside left jacket pocket, with the fake thumb resting on top of it. The thumbcuffs and keys should go in your outside right jacket pocket.

Figure 2

The Secret of the Thumbcuffs:
Actually, thumbcuffs are a legitimate restraint and are just as effective as police regulation handcuffs. The secret of escaping from the thumbcuffs is to make it look as if you are locked up when truly you are not. However, in the context of a magic performance, a good magician can condition the audience to believe he is completely restrained. When the cuffs are being locked onto your thumbs, simply press up against the locking mechanism so your volunteer will think the cuffs are locked on tight.

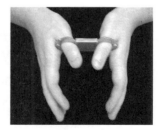
Figure 3

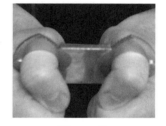
Figure 4

Arching your thumbs toward yourself helps to prevent the cuffs from being locked on too tightly (FIG. 3). Flinching and squinting will also help convince the audience that the cuffs are locked on snug. Once you are supposedly locked in, angle your thumbs outward to fill up the thumb-holes of the cuffs (FIG. 4). To escape, all you need do is pull your thumbs free from the cuffs. So as not to give anything away, you should escape only under cover of the handkerchief.

Practice by locking yourself in the cuffs. Listen to the teeth of the locking mechanism click as the cuffs are locked onto your thumbs (FIG. 5). Count the exact number of clicks that you can withstand and still free yourself. Knowing the exact number of clicks will prove to be useful information in an actual performance. Good luck.

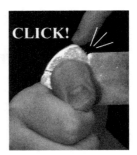

Figure 5

I. Introduction

Introduce the thumbcuffs to your audience. Most or all of your audience has probably never seen a pair of thumbcuffs. Explain how the cuffs work and what they are used for. *Being a magician, I have to tell little white lies constantly. To keep a straight face while doing this, I have found it best to stick as close to the truth as possible.* Inform your audience, "Thumbcuffs are generally used by police who are undercover, such as the FBI. Undercover police prefer to use thumbcuffs because they are less bulky and are just as effective as handcuffs." Call upon a female volunteer at this time. Say, "Come closer, ma'am. Allow me to show you how they work."

Why call on a female assistant? There are several reasons you should pick a lady to help with this particular routine. Ladies in general are more polite and cooperative than men when called on to help during magic routines. Shortly, you will need someone to lock you into the cuffs. A woman is less likely to try to spoil your routine or upstage you. And it is always beneficial to have a lovely assistant at your side when performing magic; ask any illusionist. Be sure to choose a woman who has a fun spirit about her if you want to create an unforgettable performance.

II. Proving a Point

After a lady has come up to help, slip the cuffs onto her thumbs and lock them down tight. You do not want her to slip out of the cuffs, and besides, she will be out of them shortly. At this point shout, "Escape from the cuffs!" Your thumbcuffed volunteer will try to escape, but to no avail. You do this, not to make her look stupid, but rather to verify that the cuffs are escape-proof. Now is a perfect moment to act as if you have misplaced or lost the keys.

If I am performing at an all-adult event, and the audience seems rowdy, then I'll do this next bit. Pull out a cat-of-nine-tails whip (FIG. 6) and say, "Now I'm gonna need you to bend over" as you strike the whip against the palm of your hand. The audience will roar. When you think about it, there is something masochistic about being tied up with a rope or locked in a restraint.

Figure 6

Note that I say nothing risqué, yet I imply what all of the perverts in the audience are thinking. I know I am walking a thin line here, but I never cross it. Use the whip gag if you think it fits your audience.

III. "Lock Me in Tight."

Produce the keys and unlock your assistant. Ask her to hold the cuffs and the keys. Push up your sleeves and remove the handkerchief from your pocket while **Finger Palming** the fake thumb in your right hand (FIG. 7). Allow the handkerchief to unfold, show it, and place it aside. Maintaining the Finger-Palmed fake thumb, make your hands into two fists, placing them side by side, and extend your thumbs (FIG. 8).

Figure 7

Ask your assistant to lock the cuffs onto your thumbs. As she does this, remember to arch your thumbs back. Press up against the locking mechanism of the cuffs as she pushes down so the thumbcuffs will appear to be on tight. Your audience should be convinced that the cuffs are secure and tight. Remember to grumble a few choice words under your breath. Do not overact here, or you will lose your audience's trust. You want your audience to show empathy about the predicament that you have put yourself into.

Figure 8

IV. "Ouch! They're Too Tight!"

Ask your assistant to cover your hands with the handkerchief. Say, "Now you know why I call this the FBI Trick, because I do it undercover." The audience groans. Grumble and complain that the cuffs are on too tight. Slip the fake thumb onto one of your thumbs under the cover of the handkerchief. Insist that your assistant must remove the cloth and loosen the cuffs. As she removes the cloth, hold your locked hands high for all to see the swollen thumb (FIG. 9).

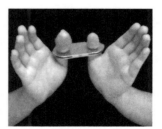

Figure 9

The audience will not be sure whether to laugh or turn their heads at this gruesome sight. To make sure your assistant doesn't feel bad, explain, "The thumb is fake." Say, "Will you please remove it?" Unsure, she will slowly approach the fake thumb. As soon as she touches it, scream loudly enough for all to hear you. Everyone will jump. Remove the thumb and toss it aside.

V. "Straighten the Handkerchief, Please."

Assuming your volunteer hasn't fled to her seat yet, ask her to cover your hands with the handkerchief again. Once you are covered, pretend to try to escape from the cuffs. Moving your hands under the cloth, position the handkerchief so it hangs more to one side. Slip your right hand out of the cuffs from under the cloth, and straighten the handkerchief while asking the assistant, "Will you please straighten the handkerchief?" Upon her compliance, the audience will explode with laughter.

Place your right hand's thumb back into the cuffs. Your assistant will most likely have no idea that you were ever free. She will then look to you for justification of the audience's reactions. The best thing to do is look at her as if you are just as confused as she is. Also, to preoccupy her mind, you might ask her to straighten the handkerchief once again.

VI. "Time Me."

Allow the handkerchief to fall from your hands, revealing that you are still locked up (FIG. 10). Ask your assistant to cover your hands with the cloth. As soon as she does this, slip your left hand free from under the handkerchief. Say, "If you would, please, time me to see how long it takes me to escape." As you say this, look at your wristwatch on your left arm, implying that she should do the same.

Figure 10

Succumbing to your demands, she will begin timing you. The spectators will squirm in their seats, trying to maintain their composure and trying not to laugh.

VII. The Vanish

Place your left hand's thumb back into the cuffs and allow the handkerchief to fall to the ground once more. This will be the last time the audience sees the thumbcuffs. Say, "I'm sorry. Will you please cover my hands again? Don't stop timing me." Once she covers your hands, remove your left hand again, and straighten the handkerchief, saying, "How am I doing on time?"

as you look at your watch. The audience giggles, and perhaps by now even your assistant is wise to what has been going on.

Regardless, place your left hand under the handkerchief and remove the thumbcuffs from your right thumb. Clip the cuffs between the index and middle finger of your right hand (FIG. 11). With your right hand's thumb, grasp the right back corner of the handkerchief, concealing the thumbcuffs underneath (FIG. 12). Keep both hands under the cloth and about 12 inches from your waist as you prepare to hide the cuffs.

Figure 11

Open your left hand palm up under the cloth to make it look full. Move your left hand toward the audience while your right hand pulls the handkerchief toward your body. Secretly, under cover of the cloth, place the cuffs into your right jacket pocket (FIG. 13). Once the cuffs are concealed, move your right arm to the extreme right. Your open left hand should still be covered with the handkerchief at this point. Whisk away the handkerchief, revealing an empty left hand.

Figure 12

Toss the cloth into the air and catch it with your left hand. This is an excellent way to say, nonverbally, "Look. My hands and the cloth are empty." Be sure to applaud your volunteer for her assistance, and the audience is sure to do the same for both of you.

Figure 13

Place all of the items back into their correct pockets to start again, and you can easily repeat this effect while strolling through a crowd.

The FBI Trick is a great routine for teaching a magician about timing and cues. As you perform this routine, you should become accustomed to each phase of the routine. Experience will teach you what audiences will say before they say it, when they will laugh, and when they will be surprised. Although the routine will be predictable in your eyes, you should be genuine in your actions and reactions each time you perform this.

Remember always to treat your volunteers with care and respect. Do not insult or intimidate a volunteer, or your performance is sure to turn into a fiasco. During this particular routine, the audience laughs for reasons unknown to the volunteer. You must comfort the volunteer with your manner and remain polite at all times. Once the routine is over, it is a nice gesture on your part to give your female volunteer a memento of your performance together.

♦ *Give her a rose.*
♦ *Give her an autographed photo of yourself.*
♦ *Give her the whip and say, "I'll see you after the show."*

Paperweight

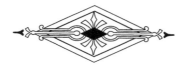

"Trust ivrybody—but cut th' ca-ards."
Finley Peter Dunne
Mr. Dooley's Philosophy

<u>Effect</u>: The magician claims that any true cardman can weigh and count the number of cards he is holding by touch alone. He demonstrates this by having a stack of cards cut from a tabled deck. Holding the cut-off portion of cards in his hand, he calls out a number. Amazingly, the same number of cards is then counted onto the table. This can be repeated several times.

I have used this effect to fool lay audiences and magicians alike. The routine seems void of any trickery whatsoever. The cards are not marked. There is no awkward handling of the pack. And the lay audience is free to cut and count the cards during the effect. How is it done? The cards are **stacked** into the **Si Stebbins System** order.

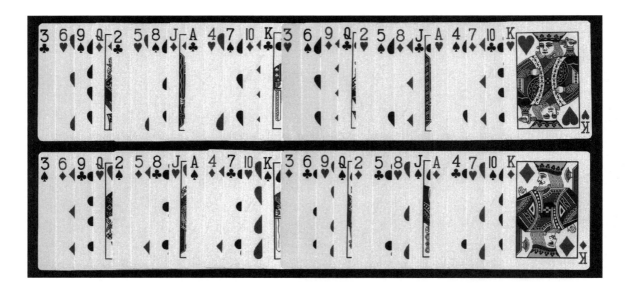

Figure 1- Si Stebbins System Order

Note: In the above card arrangement the King of Hearts is immediately followed by the Three of Spades. If and when the pack is legitimately cut, the system still works.

Routine: Prepare the deck in Si Stebbins order (FIG. 1). You may want to cut the deck or give it some **false shuffles** while explaining what you are about to do. Be sure to cut a King to the face of the deck. The King's value is thirteen, and its importance will become apparent shortly.

Place the stacked deck on the table. Say to a spectator, "Cut off any number of cards and hand them to me. I will weigh the packet and tell you exactly how many cards I am holding." As you take the stack from the spectator who cut the pack, secretly **glimpse** at the card on the face of the stack. Pretend to weigh the cards in your hand as you work the following formula in your head. Let's assume the card cut to is an Eight by studying the following example:

Bottom Card (King)	13
Subtract Cut Card (8)	- 8
Difference	5
Multiply by Four	x 4
Total	20
Add or Subtract Thirteen If Needed.	(13)
Grand Total	?

Subtract the cut card's value from the King (ex: 13 - 8 = 5). Obviously, you want the King on the face of the deck, since it holds the highest value in the Si Stebbins System. If a King is on the face of the deck, you can subtract any card's value from it. You will always multiply the difference by four (ex: 5 x 4 = 20). *This sum may or may not leave you with the exact total of cards you are holding.*

You add or subtract the value of thirteen as needed. For instance, if the cut-off stack looks as if it is less than the (ex: 20) cards, then subtract thirteen, (ex: 20 - 13 = 7). You would be holding seven cards. If it looks as if you are holding more than the (ex: 20) cards, then you would add thirteen (ex: 20 + 13 = 33). If it looks as if you are holding more than the (ex: 33) cards, then add thirteen again (ex: 33 + 13 = 46).

As you practice using this formula, it will become more obvious what to do. Do not just depend on arithmetic. Use your eyes to estimate how many cards you are holding. Knowing there are fifty-two cards in the deck will make it easier to guess how many cards have been cut. If someone cuts fewer than half of the cards from the deck, then you know that he holds fewer than twenty-six cards (52/2 = 26).

What if a King is cut? (Ex: 13 - 13 = 0, 0 x 4 = 0). Each card of a particular value is thirteen cards away from another like it. So if he does cut to a King, then he will be holding a multiple of thirteen. He will be holding thirteen, twenty-six or thirty-nine cards. You should be able to judge how many cards he has cut by the size of the packet he is holding.

What if the spectator wants to know how many cards remain on the table instead of the number of cards that were cut? Simply subtract the calculated number of cards that were cut from the deck's total of fifty-two cards (Ex: 52 - 20 = 32). The difference that is calculated should equal the number of cards on the table.

When counting the cards to reveal their number, be careful not to reverse their order. The cards must remain in Si Stebbins order if you wish to repeat the effect. There are a few ways to count and keep the cards in Si Stebbins order:

◆ Hold the stack face down and count them from the top, face up, one at a time, in a squared packet onto the table.
◆ Turn the packet face up in your hand. Now count them from the top, turning them face down, one at a time, into a squared packet onto the table.
◆ Hold the cards face down. Count them off the top or bottom of the stack, face down, one at a time, into the other hand or onto the table. As you count off the cards into the other hand, be careful not to reverse their order.

I prefer the third method, since it does not reveal the obvious red-black order of the Si Stebbins System.

Once you have finished the effect, place the cut-off packet on top of the tabled stack, completing the deck. The trick can now be repeated. It is customary that a magician should not repeat his tricks. Yet the strength of the Paperweight routine is that the magician, time and time again, accurately guesses the number of cards that were cut. *I like to perform this effect at least three times.*

The first magic book I ever bought, when I was five years old, came from a magic shop at Disney World. It is titled Magic with Cards *by Frank Garcia and George Schindler. The book transformed a boy who was fascinated with cards into a magician who could fascinate others with cards. The book taught me many amazing effects, including the trick you have just read.*

The original title of this trick was Instant Counting. I took the liberty of changing the title and the handling of this mind-blowing routine to fit my style. I believe, unbeknownst to the authors, there were several mistakes in the original explanation. My version, Paperweight, corrects these mistakes and elaborates on the use of the Si Stebbins formula. I hope you enjoy the effect as much as I have!

Finger Ring and String

"Everything that deceives may be said to enchant."
Plato
The Republic

Effect: A borrowed ring penetrates a string, vanishes from sight and reappears at will for the magician.

This has been my pet routine since 1986. I have had the privilege of watching this effect evolve over time. People love this trick for its simplicity. With a string and a borrowed ring, many have been convinced that I am the best sleight-of-hand artist they will ever see. Using my good looks, my charm, my wit, and obviously my B. S., I have booked many shows with the help of my Ring and String routine. I pass this legacy on to you.

Required Items:
♦ A ring
♦ A string

The string should be as durable as a shoestring. *I prefer to use a leather lace approximately 45 inches in length.* The leather lace can be found at any good art-supply store. The ring that you use should easily slip onto your ring finger yet appear to be snug.

Borrowing a ring: *I prefer to borrow a man's class ring or a similar type of ring. Class rings have the right weight for this effect. Rings that are not heavy enough are more difficult to manipulate with sleight of hand. Since class rings are generally big, the effect is easier for the audience to follow.*

In my opinion, you should not borrow a woman's ring for this effect. Some women's rings have precious stones in them. Imagine giving a woman back her ring in the same condition and being accused of losing a stone. And imagine dropping a lady's ring and dislodging a stone. Save yourself the heartache and borrow a man's class ring or bring your own. During this routine you must secretly place the borrowed ring onto your finger. Since most women have petite hands, it makes sense to borrow a man's ring.

Obviously, you could use your own ring for this effect. Unfortunately, using your own ring diminishes the effect somewhat. If you do use your own ring, then you must allow the audience to examine it thoroughly. No matter how closely members of the audience examine your ring, they will never be completely convinced that your ring is ordinary after they witness the full Ring and String routine. Borrow a man's ring if you can, but be prepared by having a solid-band finger ring on your person.

Why use a long string? *Most magicians who perform this trick use a much shorter string. I've found the effect looks larger and plays for a bigger crowd if a long string is used. Two people at the opposite ends of a large table can assist you by holding the ends of a long string. Several times during this routine, your guilty hand must hold one end of the string while magic is occurring at the opposite end of the string. Since the string is long, your hands will not have to be close to one another, and you can direct the audience's attention exactly where you'll need it to be.*

The Routine:

I. Penetration, Vanish and Reappearance

Present the leather string for your audience to examine while you borrow a man's ring. Take the string back and thread it through the ring. While your right hand holds the ends of the string, allow the ring to hang in the center of the string. *I usually start by saying, "All you have to do is watch the ring. My job is the hard part."*

Figure 1

The ring should be in the center of the string as you lay it into the palm of your left hand. Release the ends of the string with your right hand. An end of the string should lie across each side of your left hand (FIG. 1). Close your left hand into a loose fist around the ring on the string. Turn your left hand's fist so that your thumb is on top (FIG. 2). Use the little finger of your left hand to hold the ring loosely on the string, so that it will not fall out of your fist.

Figure 2

Figure 3

Start with your right hand near your chest, as you approach the bottom of your left hand's fist, to grab both sides of the string. Once your right hand is an inch or so from your left hand, drop the ring from your left hand's loose fist into your right hand's cupped fingers (FIG. 3); this is a variation of the Clifton Ring Move. Grasp both sides of the string with the index finger and thumb of your right hand. Move your right hand to your right, away from your left hand, stopping as you approach two to three inches from the ends of the string (FIG. 4).

Figure 4

The previous action of stealing the ring from your left hand must be done fluidly. If you pause for a millisecond during this action, then the audience will suspect foul play. Your right hand will look less suspicious if it holds

45

the string fist up rather than fist down. Obviously you should practice this move, and the moves that follow, in front of a mirror and/or video camera. Watch your angles but do not watch your hands.

Using just your left hand, pretend to fidget with an imaginary ring in your fist. Your left hand should remain closed while you pretend to pull the ring free from the string (FIG. 5). When the center of the string falls from your left hand, this will create a magical moment for your audience. Allow your right arm to relax at your side as your left hand raises its fist chest high.

Figure 5

Open your left hand, palm out, as you say, "Magic makes it disappear!" As you say this, let the ring fall from the cupped fingers of your right hand down to the center of the hanging string. Your audience will gasp upon seeing your empty left hand. Raise your right hand high while saying, "I don't know what makes it come back." The magical reappearance of the ring on the string is sure to receive "oohs and aahs" from your audience.

II. Second Penetration
Turn to one of the audience members and say, "Watch! I'll hypnotize you." Begin to wave the ring on the string in front of this person's face. After a short while say, "Don't worry! It never works. I've been trying that for years." The audience giggles and relaxes.

Holding just the ends of the string with your left hand, allow the ring to hang freely in the center of the string. Ask, "Does it look like the ring is on the string?" "Yes," the audience replies. Reiterate: "Does it feel like it's on there?" Let someone tug on the ring and reply "yes." Respond, "It's not really on there. It's an illusion or perhaps a hologram." The audience will look at you in disbelief.

Continue to hold the ends of the string with your left hand. Approach the string with your right hand and insert its ring and middle fingers between the halves of the string. Slide your right hand down toward the ring. The ring finger of your right hand should rest on the backside of the ring while its thumb touches the signet or jewel of the ring (FIG. 6). The middle and index fingers of your right hand should hold one side of the

Figure 6

string in a scissor-like grip (FIG. 7). The string and the ring should be held toward the ends of your right hand's fingers.

Figure 7

Rotate your right hand, palm up, while maintaining each finger's designated positions. As you do this, let go of the ends of the string with your left hand. Extend the index and middle fingers of your right hand outward while still holding the string (FIG. 8). Show your audience the ring is on the string as you say, "I'll hold the ends while someone holds on to the center of the string."

Figure 8

In one swift movement your left hand should approach your right hand from underneath while going in between each half of the hanging string. Commence by passing the thumb of your left hand between the middle and ring fingers of your right hand (FIG. 9). The string should be touching the top of your left hand's thumb. Your left hand's other fingers should be in front of the middle and index fingers of your right hand. The part of the string closest to your audience should lie against the back of your right hand's fingers.

Figure 9

As you move your left hand up and away from your right hand, the string will free itself from the ring. The thumb of your left hand will do most of the work. Turn your right hand toward yourself, as you unlace the string from the ring, to cover the move. As the end of the string leaves the ring, lift the ring on top of the center of the string, using only your right hand's thumb; this is better known as Grismer's Move. From the audience's perspective, there should be no reason to believe the ring is not on the string.

Your left hand should keep moving away from your right hand until it approaches the ends of the string. Stop and grip the ends of the string with your left hand. Your right hand should be holding the ring in a pinched-grip on top of the string. Your hands should be about a foot and a half apart (FIG. 10).

Figure 10

Reach toward a spectator on your right with your right hand while still pinching the ring and string together. Say, "Hold on to this end, and whatever you do, don't let the ring come off." As this person reaches up to hold the center of the string, let go of it with your right hand. As the string falls from your right hand, the audience will be amazed.

With your right hand, hold the ring high for all to see. Comfort the spectator by saying, "I was cheating. As you all know, I must cheat to be in this business." The audience smiles.

At this point in the routine, you can perhaps see why it was so important to borrow a ring and have the string examined. Had you not done this earlier, everyone would want to examine your props now. Stopping and starting an effect in the middle of a presentation is never recommended, because you could lose your audience or the magical moment that you've created. Besides, if your audience thinks that the ring or string is gimmicked, then you will receive no credit for being clever with your hands.

III. "Déjà Vu . . . All Over Again!"
Thread the ring back onto the center of the string. Place the ring and string in the palm of your left hand. An end of the string should lie across each side of your left hand. Close your left hand into a loose fist.

Turn your left fist down so that your audience can see only the back of your

Figure 11

left hand. The side of the string that hangs to the right of your left hand should be handed to someone on your left. The string should now be extended across the back of your left hand (FIG. 11). Command your volunteer, "Hold on to this end of the string tightly, and don't let go."

Figure 12

Pass your right hand over the back of your left hand's wrist and reach toward your left hand's fingertips. It should appear that you are reaching for the other side of the string. Actually, you should drop the ring from your left hand's loose fist into the cupped middle, ring and little fingers of your right hand (FIG. 12); this is Clifton's Ring Move. If you open your left hand's fist accidentally, you will spoil the effect. Turn your right hand palm up as you come back over your left hand's empty closed fist, with the ring **Finger Palmed** in your right hand (FIG. 13). The audience should assume you are merely grasping the string in your right hand.

Figure 13

Move your right hand along the string to your right as if you were going to hand that end of the string to someone. Slow down once you get to about an inch from the end of the string. Turn your right hand to your left, palm down, and pinch some of the string to your left between the index finger and thumb of your right hand (FIG. 14). The action of turning your right hand to your left should cause the leather lace to free itself from the ring. Do not hold the string too tightly. If the string does not pull itself free from the ring, then simply run the index finger and thumb of your right hand closer to that end of the string, and it will be forced out.

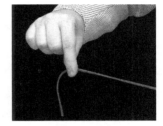

Figure 14

The beauty of the previous action is that it appears your right hand never reached the end of the string. Therefore, in your audience's mind, the ring must still be on the string held by your left hand's fist. Instruct someone nearby to hold on to that end tightly as well. Allow your right arm to hang at your side.

Turn your left hand's fist palm up as your right hand places the ring onto its ring finger. This is not as hard to do as it sounds. Since the ring is resting in Finger Palm position, use your right hand's thumb to maneuver the ring over the tip of your right hand's ring finger. Use the thumb of your right hand to push the ring onto your ring finger as far as it will go (FIG. 15).

Figure 15

Open your left hand, palm up, once the ring is completely on your right hand's ring finger. Hiding the ring from your audience, bring your right hand up in the shape of a make-believe gun (FIG. 16). Point to your open left hand with your right hand's pretend gun as you say, "Look! It's like déjà vu." Pause and then extend all of your right hand's fingers to reveal the ring. Finish the remark by saying, "All over again." Your

Figure 16

audience will be flabbergasted.

Once the members of your audience close their mouths, continue standing there to enjoy the stunned silence. It will take some of your audience members longer to realize that the ring has penetrated the string, vanished and reappeared on your finger. Let the rest of your audience catch up with the others before you continue. Applause is sure to follow this brief silence. Timing is everything here, so do not rush it.

IV. Retention Vanish & Reappearance

Put the string aside for a moment. Slip the ring off your right hand's ring finger with help from your left hand. Exaggerate a little by acting as if the ring is difficult to remove from your finger. Place the ring into your open right hand. Prepare to perform the **Retention of Vision Vanish** with the ring (FIG. 17).

Figure 17

Execute the Retention of Vision Vanish with the ring as you say, "Did you know that the ring has a hole in it?" Using your left hand's fist, reach toward someone as if you are going to hand him or her the ring. Allow your right arm to relax at your side. Slide the ring onto your right hand's ring finger, with the aid of your thumb, as you did earlier.

Declare, "Yes, it does," as you open your empty left hand for all to see. The audience will be taken aback. Raise your right hand and flash the ring to your audience. Conclude by saying, "That's how I get it onto my finger so fast." After that cute remark, some will laugh out loud while others may laugh on the inside.

V. Finale

Exclaim, "I know that some of you are thinking, 'I wish he'd do that just once again.' Guess what? I'm gonna do it one more time *in slow motion*." Remove the ring from your right hand's ring finger with the help of your left hand. Grip the ring between the index finger and thumb of your left hand. The jewel of the ring should be facing you. Hold the ring as shown in FIG. 18.

Figure 18

Pick up the string with your right hand. About five inches of the string should hang over the index finger of your right hand and lie across the front of its fingers. The remainder of the string should lie across the back of your right hand's fingers. Your right hand's thumb should pinch the string against your right hand's index finger to prevent it from falling (FIG. 19).

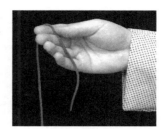

Figure 19

Extend the middle, ring and little fingers of your left hand upward while still holding the ring in a pinched-grip with your left hand's outstretched index finger and thumb (FIG. 20). With the aid of your right hand, insert the shorter end of the string into the ring. Your right hand's fingers should pass between the index and middle fingers of your left hand. The main length of the string should lie against the back of the ends of your left hand's extended fingers (FIG. 21).

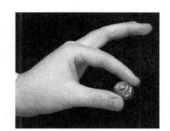

Figure 20

Your left hand should remain still as your right hand continues moving in a downward motion. Once the string is free from the ring, pivot your left hand toward the audience as you relax the middle, ring and little fingers of your left hand. All of your left hand's fingers should be extended out straight and parallel to one another. The thumb and fingers of your left hand should keep the ring positioned on top of the center of the string (FIG. 22). From the audience's perspective, the ring should appear to be threaded on the string.

Figure 21

Figure 22

Use your left hand's thumb to push the ring in between its middle and ring finger. A small part of the string should be caught under the ring (FIG. 23). At this point, when someone looks at the ring from above, it's perceived that the ring is threaded onto the string. The illusion is not absolutely angle-proof, so watch the position of your left hand.

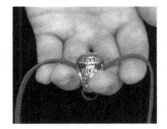

Figure 23

Say, "To add an extra level of difficulty, I will tie a knot around the ring." Use your right hand to tie an actual knot around the ring. Hand two volunteers each a separate end of the string and instruct them to "pull tight and don't let go." Everyone should be convinced the ring could not possibly come off the knotted string.

As the two volunteers tighten the knot, pull your left hand back toward yourself. Concentrate on pinching the string between the middle and ring fingers of your left hand. Use your left hand's thumb to hold the ring in place. Pull your left hand back as far as you can without letting go of the string, in order to create tension on it. Prepare the audience for the finale by warning them: "Don't blink or you'll miss it."

Snap your fingers as loudly as you can with your right hand. As your snap echoes through the room, release the string from your left hand's pinched grip. As the string shoots forward, use your left hand's thumb to position the ring on top of its fingers. These theatrics will create an everlasting image for all to remember. Your audience should be stunned.

Chances are that many will want to examine the props again, so let them. The skeptics in the crowd will want to find a secret compartment in the ring or string, hoping to debunk you. More than likely, after the skeptics fail to find any smoke or mirrors, one of them will insist, "Do it again!" Do not bow to their commands. Just say something witty like, "Good magicians will not repeat their tricks, and neither will I." Always leave your audience wanting more.

To receive the maximum impact for this effect, push up your sleeves. You and I both know that you don't need long sleeves for this effect. However, your audience does not know it. The crowd loves it when I push up my sleeves when I'm doing magic, so I accommodate them when I can.

I need to thank Dan Fleshman, the first magician I ever saw give a lecture. I was a semi-pro who had just begun to make money with magic when I attended Fleshman's lecture. Dan blew me away. All of his routines are works of art. He was the first magician I ever saw make a coin fall up or perform the classic Cups and Balls routine. It was very exciting to see a master work his craft.

My Finger Ring and String routine is a modified version of Fleshman's handling. The effect has blossomed over the years, and I really feel that I've made it my own. I have taken out pieces of Dan's routine, and added pieces of my own, to create an effect that works for me. I hope you will do the same.

Soaring Straw

*"Every man takes the limits of his own field
of vision for the limits of the world."*
Arthur Schopenhauer
Parerga and Paralipomena

Effect: An ordinary drinking straw mysteriously moves from one of the magician's hands to the other. Then the straw magically jumps from hand to hand. One hand is held high, and the straw magically floats up into it. This is truly a spectacle for the audience to behold.

There are two well-known floating effects on the market that close-up magicians love to perform. One effect is the Floating Bill, of which there are many versions. The other effect is Steve Duscheck's Wunderbar. The wonder of the Wunderbar effect is that a small metallic bar floats to and from a corked glass test tube. Whereas the Floating Bill is just that, a dollar bill that floats in midair. *Wanting to do something unique in restaurants, I came up with the Soaring Straw idea.*

Similar to the Wunderbar, the straw seems to come to life, as opposed to the Floating Bill, which stays frozen in midair. The use of a straw makes logical sense in a restaurant. When you use a clear straw for this routine, the audience can concentrate on the magic rather than the method behind the effect. Try this. You'll love it!

Required Items:
♦A pair of scissors
♦Some Scotch® or invisible tape
♦Some drinking straws. *I prefer the clear kind.*
♦Some magician's **invisible thread**. *In my opinion, magician John Kennedy's Fine Invisible Thread is the best on the market.*

(For illustrative purposes, I have used a regular white drinking straw and a thick black string.)

Tips when performing (effects with invisible thread) E.W.I.T.:

DO:
♦Work over a white surface when preparing E.W.I.T.
♦Place tape on the ends of the thread when preparing E.W.I.T.
♦Use a magnifying glass if possible when preparing E.W.I.T.

DO NOT:
♦Perform E.W.I.T. outside in the sunlight, or you will reveal the method.
♦Perform E.W.I.T. near a window where sunlight shines through.
♦Perform E.W.I.T. against a solid color background, or the thread will be visible to some of the audience.

Preparation: Begin by removing a single strand of invisible thread from its packaged bundle. Wrap a piece of Scotch tape around each end of the single thread. Place tape on the ends to make it easier to know exactly where the thread is. The thread will probably be at least a couple of feet long. Later, you will cut or break the thread to the exact length that you need to perform the Soaring Straw routine.

Tie one end of the thread around the center of the straw. Securing the thread is easier said than done, since it is fragile and practically invisible. To begin, hold one end of the thread by pinching the piece of tape between your right hand's index finger and thumb. Hold your left hand up, extending only your index and middle fingers. Slowly wrap the thread around the back of your left hand's extended fingers. Open your left hand's extended fingers like a pair of scissors. Push the taped end of the thread, held by your right hand, into the opening or loop you've created (FIG. 1). Now you have made a knot.

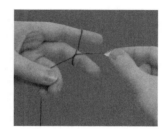
Figure 1

Slide the straw into your loosely formed knot (FIG. 2). Remove your left hand's fingers from the knot and tighten the thread around the center of the straw. Repeat this procedure two or three more times to ensure that the knots are secure and tight. The short piece of thread that remains should be cut off and discarded.

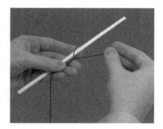
Figure 2

You should have a long piece of invisible thread with a piece of tape at one end and a straw tied to the other. Be sure the thread is positioned in the exact center of the straw. When you hold the straw up by the taped end of the invisible thread, it should remain perfectly balanced in the air. If it does not, adjust the thread until the straw is balanced.

With the straw balanced properly, adjust the length of the thread. The thread needs to be the same length as the distance between your elbow and your fingertips (FIG. 3). Hold the thread up to your forearm and break it off at the proper length. Discard the top piece that has been broken off and wrap tape around the new end of the thread.

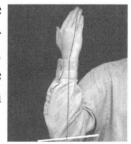
Figure 3

Double the tape upon itself along with the end of the thread.

Wrap a few pieces of tape around the end of the thread, creating a small wad. The small wad should be the size of a small pea. For storage purposes, roll the straw between your fingers, winding the thread around the straw. Tuck the small wad of tape into one end of the straw for safekeeping. Make several of these gimmicked straws at one time so they will be ready when you need them.

Before beginning the routine, you must unwind the thread from around the gimmicked straw. Place the small wad of tape, which is on the opposite end of the straw, into your mouth. Keep the tape-wad between your cheek and gum on one side of your mouth. With the thread hanging from your mouth, you will feel some tension on your bottom lip from the weight of the straw.

Place the gimmicked straw into your shirt or jacket breast pocket. *Performing in a strolling environment, where I must carry several effects on my person, I've found that my outer breast jacket pocket is the best place to keep the gimmicked straw. One, the protruding drinking straw can be concealed under my jacket's lapel. Two, keeping the gimmicked straw in the outer breast pocket leaves the loose-hanging invisible thread on the outside of my jacket. Now my hands are free to go into my jacket to retrieve other items without any fear of breaking the thread.*

Routine:

I. Walking the Straw

Prepare for the effect by secretly placing the wad of tape between your cheek and gum. Standing and facing your audience, carefully remove the gimmicked straw from your breast pocket with your right hand. Place your left hand palm up about waist high and lean slightly forward. Lay the straw in the center of your left hand so that one of the ends points toward yourself and the other end points toward your audience. Move your left hand toward the audience as you place your right hand palm up between your body and your moving left hand (FIG. 4). The straw should seem to walk into your right hand.

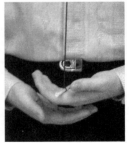

Figure 4

Repeat this action by moving your right hand toward the audience while placing your left hand between your body and your moving right hand. As you do this each time, you must move one hand under the other so not to become entangled with the thread (FIG. 5). Keep repeating this maneuver with your hands to create the illusion of the straw walking on its own. Practice this until you have the rhythm perfected.

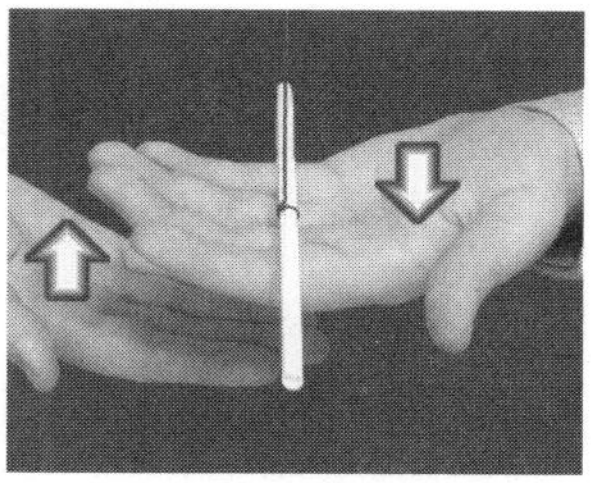

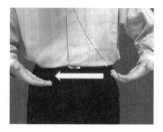
Figure 5

II. Making the Straw Jump from Hand to Hand
Assuming the straw is in your left hand, move the left hand toward the audience until it is approximately eight inches from your waist. Lean slightly farther forward as you move the straw and hand outward. As you look down, it should appear as if your left hand is just in front of your feet. You must lean forward to keep the straw away from your body and execute the jumping move successfully.

To create the illusion of the straw jumping from hand to hand, move your left hand to your extreme left. The straw hanging from the thread will want to swing to your right (FIG. 6). Let the straw leave your left hand as it swings to your right. Allow the straw to land in your right hand. Repeat this maneuver with your right hand, allowing the straw to swing to your left. Catch the straw in your left hand and repeat the jumping move a few more times.

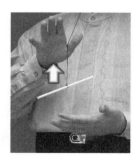
Figure 6

III. Making the Straw Float Upward
Assuming the straw is in your left hand, move the straw in the hand directly in front of you. You should lean forward with your left hand at waist level. Move your right hand up to chest level and turn your hand so it is palm down. Your right hand should remain between the hanging thread and your chest, with its fingers extended.

Move your open right hand toward the audience until the thread rests against the crotch of the thumb and index finger. As you move your right hand out toward the audience, the straw will levitate upward (FIG. 7). Keep moving your right hand outward until the straw contacts the palm of your right hand. When the straw finally meets your right hand, simply grasp it and place it back into your shirt or jacket breast pocket. The mouths of your audience members are sure to be agape.

Figure 7

Never allow the straw to hang in midair, or you might tip the method. Keeping the straw and your hands constantly moving convinces the audience there are no threads used during the effect. Any time a magician causes an inanimate object to come to life, the audience will be awestruck. There are many examples of this in magic, such as the **Zombie Ball***, the* **Haunted Matchbox***, the* **Dancing Handkerchief***, etc. The investment you make in the Soaring Straw effect should be only pennies. However, the looks of amazement and comments you receive from your audience while performing this effect are priceless.*

Comedy Shuffling Routine

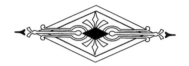

*"Imagine the Creator as a stand-up comedian—
and at once the world becomes explicable."*
H. L. Mencken

<u>Effect</u>: The magician gives the audience a quick and amusing overview of the art of shuffling cards.

<u>Required Items</u>: You'll need a deck of good-quality cards. *Don't worry about it being a full deck. I never play with a full deck of cards. Ha, ha!*

Figure 1

<u>Routine</u>: As you take out a pack of cards, ask, "Do you play cards?" After the spectator responds, exclaim, "I'm trying to quit. I'm down to about three packs a day." The audience laughs as you place a card against your upper arm. Continue by saying, "I've been wearing those card patches and chewing that card gum." Let this idea sink in, and say, "They're supposed to help." *I hope I don't have to explain the humor in this. Just do it, and they'll laugh. I promise.*

Figure 2

Hand someone the pack and ask him or her to shuffle the cards. After the volunteer does so, return the pack and insist, "Now will you please put them back into the order that I had them in?" The audience snickers.

Inform the audience that there are many ways to shuffle cards. Execute the **Dovetail Shuffle** as you say, "One way is the Dovetail Shuffle" (FIG. 1). Finish the shuffle by performing the **Bridge** and saying, "This is the Bridge" (FIG. 2).

Figure 3

Say, "Here's one commonly known as the Overhand Shuffle." Execute the **Overhand Shuffle** (FIG. 3). Further explain, "Here's another called the Hindu Shuffle." Execute a **Hindu Shuffle** (FIG. 4).

Figure 4

Now ask, "Have you ever heard of the Russian Shuffle?" **Spring the cards** as you say, "See, there is one card *rushing* after the other" (FIG. 5). The audience is amused and impressed. Continue by stating, "I can do the Russian Shuffle behind my back." Place the cards behind you, over your shoulder, just under your neck.

Figure 5

Begin **riffling** with your thumb, causing the cards to sound as if they were springing as before. Say, "Down to the other hand, and now, for the hard part, going back up!" The audience laughs as you repeat the same riffling action. Remove the cards from behind you and act as if you had just done the impossible.

Now ask, "Have you ever heard of the Lesta Shuffle?" Receiving a "no" for a response, ask someone, "Will you cut off a small portion of the pack?" Say, "Thank you. Now I have *less to* shuffle," and shuffle the remaining cards. The audience groans.

Say jokingly, "Here's a good one. I call it the Cow Pattie Shuffle." With your right hand, hold the pack chest high. Place your left hand palm up, about waist high, directly underneath the pack. Allow the cards in your right hand to fall in small clumps into your left hand (FIG. 6). The cards should make a plopping sound as the audience shudders.

Figure 6

Proclaim, "Now I'll do the Australian Shuffle." Hold the pack underneath the table and shuffle the cards. Your audience members will roll their eyes as you say, "See, they are *down under*."

Figure 7

Inform your audience, "Here is one I like to call the Congressional Shuffle." Act as if you are about to do a Dovetail Shuffle, but do not allow the cards to come together as you riffle the pack (FIG. 7). "See, nothing gets done this way. Makes a lot of noise, though." The audience laughs. *Instead of saying the word Congressional, use the current U.S. president's name for a stronger reaction.*

Figure 8

Call everyone's attention to your hands by boasting, "Now I'll show off a little. Here's one I like to call the Arthritic or Carpal Tunnel Shuffle." Execute a **One-Hand Shuffle** (FIG. 8). The audience is highly impressed.

Finally, say, "Here's my favorite one. I call it the Confusion Shuffle." Execute the **Slop Shuffle** (FIG. 9). "See, this really mixes the cards up. It confuses them." After righting the cards, say, "The hard part is putting the cards back into the same order." **Fan** (FIG. 10) or **Ribbon Spread** (FIG. 11) the cards, showing both sides of the deck.

Figure 9

Figure 10

Here is another gag shuffle to use in an emergency. Should you mis-shuffle, say, "That was the Michigan Shuffle. I *mished again*." It's fun to use this because people are impressed when you can recover from a mishap.

When you drop cards, you could say something such as, "Sorry, it's the first day with my new hands." If the majority of the deck ends up on the floor, go down with them. Shuffle them as if they were dominoes. This really gets a belly laugh from the audience.

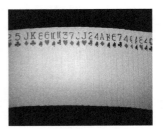
Figure 11

One last topical gag shuffle is the Probation Shuffle. Instead of saying *probation*, though, use the name of a famous sports star or team that is currently on probation. For example, say, "Here is the Dallas Cowboys Shuffle." Place the deck onto the table and say, "They're on probation!" The audience will laugh; *I promise*.

The Comedy Shuffling Routine is a great opener for any card routine that does not require the deck to be in a specific order. Add some shuffles to the routine if you like, but remember to keep the routine short and sweet. To some it might seem necessary to delete a few shuffles to keep the routine within a reasonable time frame. Actually, the routine, as is, takes only about one or two minutes to complete at a moderate pace.

Invisible Thumbscrews

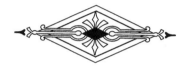

"Make the other person happy about doing the thing that you suggest."
Dale Carnegie
Principle Nine from *How to Win Friends & Influence People*

<u>Effect</u>: Using invisible thumbscrews, the magician causes the spectator's two outstretched index fingers to come together magically.

This routine was shown to me by a great magician friend to whom this book is dedicated. As a hypnotist, he used this routine to win over his subjects. It was his idea to use the invisible thumbscrews. The idea of the thumbscrews helps to make this old bit even more magical. Try this bit before another of your favorite **mentalism** *routines, and you will discover that it helps to make the magic moment much stronger.*

Figure 1

<u>Routine:</u> Have a female spectator interlace her fingers and clench them tightly into a fist. *I say, "Pretend you are squeezing the juice from a lemon"* (FIG. 1). Once the volunteer has done that for a few seconds, have her outstretch her index fingers. Instruct your subject to press her index fingers together (FIG. 2). Having done that, instruct your subject to separate her index fingers, bending the fingers back as far as they will go (FIG. 3).

Figure 2

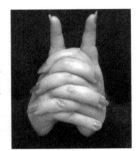

Figure 3

Now act quickly. Place the index finger and thumb of each of your hands near the back of each her outstretched index fingers (FIG. 4). Using your index fingers and thumbs, pretend to be turning a thumbscrew with each your hands. The muscles in her index fingers will relax, causing them to come together. As this happens, bring your pinched fingers in closer to narrow the area into which she can stretch her index fingers. Explain that you do not wish to touch her fingers, and she should not touch you. Continue bringing your fingers in closer as your subject's fingers relax, finally touching. Once her fingers meet, breathe a sigh of relief, and act as if this were difficult to accomplish.

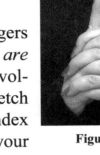

Figure 4

Obviously, when you perform the Invisible Thumbscrews, you want to select someone who will cooperate and follow instructions. Yet if she should try to resist, remind her again to relax and not to touch you. Eventually, your subject's fingers will relax and you can move your fingers inward, subconsciously pushing hers together. If you are polite, she will want the trick to work. People love to experience magic and therefore should succumb to your suggestions.

Cat and Mouse

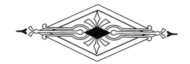

"In the theater the audience wants to be surprised—
but by things that they expect."
Tristan Bernard
Contes, repliques et bon mots

<u>Effect</u>: A selected card is mixed back into the deck. A mousetrap is intro-
duced and set. Cards are then randomly put into the trap. Amazingly, the
trap does not go off until the selected card is placed on the trigger.

Required Items:
- ◆ A pencil
- ◆ A mousetrap
- ◆ A deck of cards
- ◆ A permanent marker

<u>Preparation</u>: You will need to loosen the spring-arm of the mousetrap. Do this by using your fingers or a tool to bend the arm back (FIG. 1). You want the arm to be just strong enough to make the trap work properly. However, you do not want the spring action to be strong enough to hurt anyone, should a participant's fingers or yours get caught in the trap. Set the trap and test it by placing a pencil on the trigger. Use common sense here.

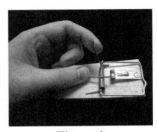

Figure 1

During this effect you will be **forcing** a card. *I prefer to use the **Hindu Shuffle Force***. You will need to be able to locate the card from its back. To locate the **force card** (ex: 7◆) from the back side, place pencil dots in the upper-left-hand and lower-right-hand corners of the card (FIG. 2). Make the pencil dots just dark enough that only you can notice them. Place the force card on the face of the deck, and you are ready to begin.

Figure 2

For the effect's finale, you will predict the chosen card. With your permanent marker, print on the back side of the mousetrap:

Figure 3

CAUTION!
When Inserting the Seven of Diamonds,
Keep Fingers Out!

<u>Routine</u>: Begin by forcing the 7◆ using the Hindu Shuffle Force (FIG. 3). Continue to Hindu Shuffle cards off the top of the pack and onto the cards in your left hand (FIG. 4). Stop once the force card is within the top ten cards of the pack, and assemble the deck.

Figure 4

Now bring out the mousetrap, and explain that you are going to play a little game of cat-and-mouse with the cards. Set the trap, treating it gingerly, as if it were truly dangerous to handle. I usually joke, *"Kids, don't try this at home! Make sure you go over to your friend's house to try it."* The audience grins.

Once the trap is set, remove the top card, face down, from the deck. Holding the card with a soft grip, lightly touch the card to the trigger of the mousetrap (FIG. 5). The trap should not go off. By loosening the spring-arm, you have made the trigger less sensitive. Turn the card face up onto the table as you say, "That's not it." Wince and shrug as you place cards on the trigger. Continue doing this with cards until you notice the pencil-dot force card on top of the pack.

Figure 5

Remove the force card from the top of the pack. Grip the card firmly by pinching it between the index finger and thumb. The pressure that you apply should extend the full length of the card, making it rigid. Push the card onto the trigger as shown in FIG. 5. This time you should press the trigger downward with the card. The trap will go off.

After the excitement, press down on the U-shaped metal arm of the contraption as you pick the mousetrap up. Act as if the card is stuck in the trap, and pull it free. Flip the card over and say, "Just as I thought." Reveal the prediction on the back side of the mousetrap. The audience will be amazed and amused. The amazement comes from discovering that the "caught card" is also the selected card. The amusement comes from reading the prediction on the back of the trap.

This routine may not be a show-stopper, but it does have entertainment value. Each time you touch a card to the trigger of the mousetrap, the members of your audience will be on the edges of their seats. When the trap goes off, there is silent jubilation felt by all. Finally, when the selection and prediction are revealed, everyone has a good laugh. Just like a good movie, the Cat and Mouse routine provides excitement, fear, wonder, and ultimately laughter.

Fireball

You see things; and you say, "Why?" But I dream
things that never were; and I say, "Why not?"
George Bernard Shaw
Back to Methuselah

Effect: The magician shows a large square white piece of tissue paper. He tears the paper into fourths and wads the pieces into a ball. He places the paper ball onto the end of a large needle. He ignites the pieces, creating a huge spontaneous fireball. Magically, the fire goes out and the paper is shown to be whole again. This is a breath-taking effect to watch and perform.

Required Items:

♦ A pair of scissors
♦ A pair of safety goggles or wacky sunglasses
♦ An 8½-inch square packet of **flash paper**. *Flash paper is sold in most magic shops. I prefer to use flash paper that has not been folded.*
♦ White tissue paper *such as the kind that comes with your dry cleaning*
♦ A large needle *such as the one included with the* **Needle Thru Balloon** *effect, which is also sold in most magic shops.*
♦ Something to ignite the paper with, such as matches, a lighter, a lit candle, etc.

Preparation: Although the flash paper you will be using is 8½ inches square, you will need to prepare a larger piece of tissue paper for the switch. The reason the tissue paper should be larger is that it will be wadded into a ball and then unfolded later. Once the tissue is unfolded it will appear smaller. Cut a 10-inch-square piece from the white tissue and fold it diagonally in half, forming a triangle.

Figure 1

Twist the two opposite ends of the paper triangle into a small wad, creating two small handles (FIG. 1). These are the handles you will use to undo the paper ball. Wad the paper into a ball, allowing the two handles to protrude. Finish by compressing the paper ball with handles to the size of a large gumball (FIG. 2).

Figure 2

Presentation: Ask your audience, "Have you ever seen a magician perform the classic effect where a newspaper is torn into pieces and then magically restored?" After their response, say, "Usually the effect is done on TV or on a stage. I'll perform the effect up close so you can see and hear the paper being torn." Reach into your jacket, table or case with your right hand and **Finger Palm** the balled-up piece of tissue. Use your right hand to bring out the square piece of flash paper as well (FIG. 3).

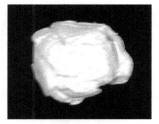

Figure 3

To make your right hand less suspicious, grip the paper the same way with your left hand. Hold the flash paper near the top and center and tear it in half. As you tear the paper, move your hands slowly and meticulously so that your audience will assume all is fair. Square the two pieces and tear them in half again. Fan two pieces in each hand, revealing the four pieces to your audience (FIG. 4).

Figure 4

Square the four pieces and wrap them around the finger palmed paper ball in your right hand. Your audience should think that you are crumpling the pieces into a ball. Hold the ball in a pinched-grip between the thumb and index finger of your left hand. Be sure that the ball never leaves the audience's sight, and make the audience aware of it.

Remove the large needle and push the paper ball onto the end of it. Proclaim, "I need my safety goggles!" Place the needle in your left hand as your right hand retrieves your sunglasses or safety goggles. Put on your safety goggles as you say, "I intend to weld the pieces back together." Your audience should smile as it scoots back.

I like to say, "Kids, don't play with fire unless you want to look really cool." That line always produces a mixed yet humorous reaction. Bring out something to ignite the paper ball. Wave the flame around the ball to create suspense (FIG. 5).

Figure 5

Before you set the ball on fire, make sure your left hand is holding the opposite end of the needle, away from the paper ball. Move your left arm away from your body, and your audience, as you prepare to touch the flame to the ball. Touch the flame to the ball and then immediately pull your right hand away. A huge spontaneous flame will be produced, creating gasps from your audience. The fire should put itself out. If not, then blow it or pat it out quickly.

Put away your match or lighter. Remove your safety goggles and put them aside. Pull the ball from the end of the needle and place the needle aside. Allow your audience's eyes to regain their focus as you say, "I believe I've done it!" Find the two twisted paper handles and pull them away from one another (FIG. 6). This usually produces another gasp from your

Figure 6

audience. As you open the crumpled paper, applause is sure to follow.

History shows that mankind has been fascinated with fire since the dawn of time. When putting together an act, I usually concentrate on the idea of variety. To give your act variety, include effects with impressive hand co-ordination, humor, suspense, etc. Fire is an excellent way to produce variety. Experience has taught me that fire demands attention and has a hypnotic effect on an audience.

My effect was fostered by another effect entitled Shriek of the Mutilated, found in one of magic's best-selling books, Impossibilia, *by John Bannon. Bannon's creation is a version of the close-up effect called the* **Cigarette Paper Tear**. *I love and still perform Bannon's original version. However, I wanted to perform the same effect, on a larger scale, in a stand-up environment. Henceforth, the brainchild, Fireball, was born.*

Mathemagic

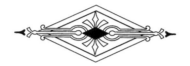

*"The knowledge of numbers is one of the chief
distinctions between us and the brutes."*
Lady Mary Wortley Montagu
From a letter (1753)

<u>Effect</u>: A packet of cards seems to grow in number while a spectator counts them in his or her own hands.

Preparation: Count fifteen cards face down into your hand or onto the table. Reverse the four bottom cards face up of the fifteen-card **packet** (FIG. 1). **Square** the packet. Bow the length of the packet by squeezing the cards end to end so that the packet arches upward (FIG. 2). Place the packet on top of the balance of the deck. Put the cards into their box, and you are ready to begin.

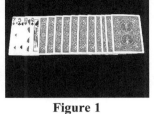

Figure 1

Bowing the fifteen cards makes it possible to cut the packet with ease from the top of the deck. You may need to practice bowing and cutting the cards until you get the hang of it. If you do not feel comfortable cutting the bowed packet from the deck, then hold a **break** *below the prepared fifteen-card packet as you begin the routine (FIG. 3). Now you can cut the cards at the break and arrive at the same result.*

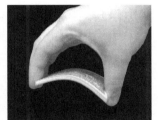

Figure 2

Routine: Remove the cards from their box and give the deck a couple of **false cuts**. Place the deck in your left hand and hold it in the **Dealer's Grip**. Looking at the length of the deck, you will notice the bow of the fifteen-card packet (FIG. 4). *Obviously, if you can see the bowed packet, so can your audience.* This is why you should hold the deck in the Dealer's Grip to conceal the long sides of the deck. The front of the deck should already be facing your audience.

Figure 3

Cut off the fifteen-card packet from the top of the deck and hand it to a spectator. Continue to hold the balance of the deck in your left hand. Without spreading the cards, have the spectator guess how many he is holding. The spectator will usually guess around fifteen cards. Exclaim, "I'm guessing that there are twenty-one cards in your hand."

Figure 4

Figure 5

Address the spectator by saying, "Count the cards by flipping the top card face up, placing it at the bottom of the packet. Count each of them out loud until you are done" (FIG. 5). Stopping at the count of eleven, the spectator will be holding a face-up stack of cards in his hands. At this point say, "Well, it appears that you were more accurate in your guess than I, but eleven cards just doesn't seem right to me. If you would, count the cards face down, one at a time, onto the table."

Figure 6

As the spectator starts counting, all attention will be on him and the cards he is holding. During this moment, discreetly thumb off the six cards from the top of the deck into your left hand (FIG. 6). Square the six cards and secretly **palm** them in your right hand (FIG. 7). Whether you are standing or sitting, allow your right arm to relax naturally and place the balance of the deck in your left hand on the table. *Do not look at your hands as you count off and palm the cards. All of your attention should appear to be focused on the spectator while he is counting the cards.*

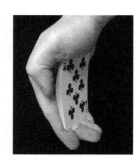

Figure 7

Once the spectator arrives at the count of fifteen cards, the audience will be surprised. With your right hand, push the stack of fifteen cards toward the spectator, loading the palmed six cards onto the stack. As you back away from the table say, "Hmm? Fifteen cards, huh? I am not sure that's right, either. Will someone please count the cards out loud once more?" Someone will now count the cards, revealing a total of twenty-one cards, to everyone's amazement. Smirk as you say, "OK, that sounds right."

On paper this routine may appear to be condescending to the spectator. However, only your demeanor toward the audience would convey that message. I choose not to belittle anyone during this routine. I simply suggest, "Why don't you try again?" in a light-hearted manner. Believe me when I say it is the conviction of the spectators that they can count correctly that makes this effect seem magical. Remember that audiences always enjoy being fooled by a gentleman.

The best thing about the Mathemagic routine is that all of the magic seems to take place in the spectator's hands. Any professional close-up magician will tell you that the best effects happen in the audience's hands. Try to work audience participation into all of your effects to make the magic moment more memorable. When you stand before a group and perform without the assistance of the audience, your effects become "bubble gum for their eyes."

The Animated Cardbox

"Reality is merely an illusion, albeit a very persistent one."
Albert Einstein

<u>Effect</u>: After performing his favorite card trick, the magician displays the cardbox in his hand. The box spins around and then stands up. Magically, the cardbox flap opens up so the magician may place the cards back inside. Upon closing the flap, the magician tosses the pack out for all to examine.

<u>Required Items:</u>
♦ A pack of good-quality cards with their box. *I prefer the Bicycle® brand of cards, but Tally-Ho®, Hoyle®, Aviator®, Bee®, or any other good brand will do.*
♦ Some clear thin monofilament. *Better known in fabric stores as Invisible Thread (FIG. 1).*
♦ A ladies' latex make-up sponge
♦ A pair of scissors

Figure 1

<u>Preparation:</u>   Remove the cards from their box. Remove the plastic wrapper from the box if you wish. Tear the small flaps from the cardbox and cut a small slit in the center of the card flap (FIG. 2).

Figure 2

While the monofilament or Invisible Thread is still on the spool, tie a knot in the thread's end. Tie a few more knots in the end of the thread in exactly the same place so that it appears to be one big knot. Cut the excess thread free from the knot. The knot will now become the new end of the thread (FIG. 3).

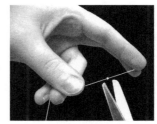

Figure 3

Hold the knotted end of the thread pinched between the index finger and thumb of your left hand. Generally, the thread needs to be the same as the length from the elbow to the fingertips. Cut the thread just a little longer than this so you'll have extra to work with. Tie the unknotted end of the Invisible Thread to a small wedge of the make-up sponge. The make-up sponge will be referred to as the *anchor* from here on.

If you are wearing a suit-jacket, then place the anchor into your right outside jacket pocket. If you are not wearing a suit-jacket, then place the anchor into your right front pants pocket. Whichever pocket you select, be sure to tuck the anchor into one of the pocket's corners so that it will remain secure. Sometimes you can place the anchor into your waist-band. After practicing and performing the effect, try placing the anchor in different positions on your body to see what works best for you. Run the prepared thread through the small slit as you approach the card flap from behind (FIG. 4). Pull the thread toward you until the knot in the end of the thread rests against the

Figure 4

slit. The knot should be resting on the blank side of the flap. Place the cards into their box and close the card flap. Place the cards into one of your right-hand pockets, along with the anchor, and you are ready to perform the effect.

Figure 5

Performance: Assuming the set-up pack is in one of your right-hand pockets, remove it with your right hand. The pack should be positioned as shown in FIG. 5. As you hold the pack in the palm of your right hand, the clear monofilament should run between your middle and ring fingers. The thread should be shielded from the audience's view by your right hand and arm.

Carefully open the cardbox and remove the cards. Do not pull the thread free from its hook-up. Cautiously place the cardbox back into the same pocket. Perform your favorite card magic routine.

After performing your mind-blowing card effect, place the pack of cards on the table. Reach into your pocket with your right hand and remove the cardbox just as you did earlier. Inform the audience, "This is my pet pack of cards." *I usually joke, "I once had a pet rock, but it got run over!"*

The box should be positioned flat in your right hand just as it was earlier (FIG. 5). The thread should run between the middle and ring finger of your right hand. The thread should be shielded from the audience's view by your right hand and arm. Extend your right arm in front of your body to keep tension on the thread. If you do not keep tension on the line of your thread hook-up, then the thread might hang down and expose the effect's method.

At this moment, some of the thread should lie between the palm of your right hand and the cardbox. The thread should be flush with the back of your right hand and arm. If you were to move your right arm toward the audience, or away from your body, the cardbox would move in your hand. This principle is about to make the cardbox perform wonders.

Bow your right hand so that the middle of your hand is stretched upward. The heel and fingers of your right hand should be stretching downward (FIG. 6). Move your right hand slowly toward the audience, or away from your body, and the box will spin a half-circle.

Figure 6

Anytime the box moves in this routine, your left hand should hover over the right hand and pretend to be responsible for the magic (FIG. 7). Wiggle the left hand's fingers and gesture as if you were truly a magician. Your eyes should be focused on the action of the box. Think of how people might act if they could move objects with their minds. Act like those people when performing this effect.

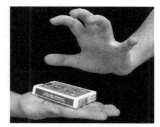

Figure 7

If you must extend your right arm too far from your body, and it seems awkward, then shorten the line by wrapping some of the thread around the anchor. *Of course you want to do this while practicing, not while performing the effect.* Once the box has spun around, use your left hand to reposition the box, as shown in FIG. 5. Make the cardbox spin a half-circle once again, and then return the cardbox to the position shown in FIG. 5 one last time.

With the aid of your left hand, roll the cardbox lengthwise until it has completely flipped over. Comment, "I'll show you the other side." Remember to keep tension on the line so it doesn't sag and reveal itself. The top of the box should be hanging over the fingertips of your right hand. The bottom of the box must be $1/4$ inch above the spot where your fingers meet your palm (FIG. 8).

Figure 8

You are about to make the box stand up. Extend your right arm slightly forward, and the box will begin to rise. As the box rises, remember to gesture as if you are willing the box to move with your left hand. *I pretend the cardbox is a real pet by clicking my tongue several times and then saying, "Come on, c'mon; that's a good boy."* Acting this way helps to focus the audience's attention on the effect and not the method. Use the thumb of your right hand to balance the box and keep it standing upright (FIG. 9). Do not allow the box to fall over.

Figure 9

Pick up the tabled deck of cards with your left hand. Say to the box, "OK, now, open up!" Move your right hand forward a little farther until the card flap pops open and extends itself backward. As the card flap begins to open, you should curl the fingers of your right hand upward to hold the box in place. Catch the card flap with your right hand's thumb and pinch it against the back of the cardbox (FIG. 10). If the card flap were to pop up after the knotted end of the thread pulled free, it might suggest to your audience that something once was connected to it.

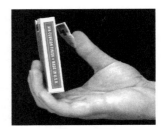

Figure 10

Place the cards in their box with your left hand. Continue to move your right arm forward slowly until the thread slips free. The thread should fall and hang at your side. Do not look at the thread. Your attention should be focused on the cards in their box.

Grab the pack with your left hand. Close the flap of the box with your right hand. Toss the pack out for all to examine. Needless to say, your audience should be in complete awe.

---

*If I were truly magical, this is one routine I think I would still perform. As far as I know, this effect is uniquely mine. If you perform the **Haunted Matchbox**, then you will recognize many similarities. In my mind, the matchbox trick is one of the best close-up routines ever created. I do believe that most card magicians would agree that the Animated Cardbox is a great closer to add to just about any card routine.*

Three Burnt Matches

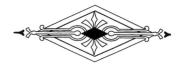

*"The best way to make a fire with two sticks
is to make sure one of them is a match."*
Will Rogers

<u>Effect</u>: The magician cons a con man out of a drink, or money, using only three burnt matches.

Working in restaurants and bars since 1986, I've met lots of characters. Once they find out I'm a magician, many of them love to try their bar bets on me. Some guys just can't refuse the chance to try to pull the wool over the eyes of someone who claims to be a master of deception. Succumbing to their bet, should I lose, I prefer to retaliate and settle the score instead of paying up. The nicest way I know of doing so is to perform this bit of business. Enjoy it!

<u>Routine</u>: Explain to the wise guy that you are about to ask him three simple questions. Tell him that if he does not answer the three questions correctly, he owes you a dollar, or whatever the bet is for. Further explain that you are going to tell him the answer to the three questions before you ask them. Take out a pack of matches and remove three of them (FIG. 1). Tell the spectator that the matches will represent the three questions that you are about to ask.

Figure 1

Light the three matches and blow them out (FIG. 2). Tell the audience that the answer to the three questions is "three burnt matches." Remind the spectator that should he respond with any other answer, he automatically loses. This sounds fair and intriguing to the audience. Usually he will accept the bet simply out of curiosity. If, however, he shows any sign of refusal to the bet, you must insist on the matter. Explain that you should at least be given a chance to recoup your loss.

Figure 2

Start by saying, "OK, first question. Let's say you had your key stuck in a door and couldn't get it out. What would you use to help?" He smiles as he replies, "Three burnt matches."

Continue, "OK, second question. Let's say you have a sore throat, and nothing that you have been taking seems to help cure it. What would you swallow to soothe your throat?" Unsure, he answers, "Three burnt matches."

Finish by saying, "OK, third and final question. What would you take in trade for a <u>dollar</u>?" Outsmarted, he replies, "Three burnt matches." *Replace the underlined phrase with whatever it is you are betting for.* Take whatever it is that you have rightfully won and give the wise guy the three burnt matches (FIG. 3).   Remember that should he refuse to answer, or answer with any other reply, you still win!

Figure 3

As a rule, magic should never be presented as a challenge if you want the audience to be on your side. However, this bit falls into the realm of bar bets and gags. Perform this gag to make money if you wish, but I prefer to use it to settle the score with a wise guy. The Three Burnt Matches routine is a nice way of saying, "Don't mess with me, buddy!"

Burning Impression

*"The mind of a man is capable of anything—because
everything is in it, all the past as well as all the future."*
Joseph Conrad
Heart of Darkness

<u>Effect</u>: The image of a selected playing card magically appears burnt into
the magician's business card.

Required Items:
- ◆ A toothpick
- ◆ A deck of cards
- ◆ A cigarette lighter
- ◆ A bottle of lemon juice concentrate
- ◆ Your own standard white business cards

Preparation: Dip the toothpick into the lemon juice and draw the image of the card to be **forced** (ex: 7♦) onto the front of your business card (FIG. 1). You must have a keen eye to do this; after all, it's like writing with invisible ink. Write the words "Your Card" lightly on the back of your business card with a pen (FIG. 2). Do not use a bold ink pen, or your message could be seen from the front of the business card, spoiling the surprise.

Figure 1

Make several of the gimmicked business cards in one sitting. The prepared business cards will last for weeks. Place the prepared cards in your pocket. Have your cigarette lighter handy. Finally, have a pack of cards, with the **force card** in position, and you are ready to begin.

Figure 2

Suggested Presentation: Tell the audience that you are about to predict the future by guessing a card soon to be selected. Place one of your prepared business cards, front side showing, onto the table for all to see. Force the desired playing card (ex: 7♦) and have the spectator show it to all present except to you, the magician. *For this effect, I prefer to use the **Break Force**.*

Ask the audience, "Would you be impressed, if your card were written on the back of my business card?" After the response, flip the business card over to reveal the words "Your Card." This comment should get a chuckle. Regardless, you are about to amaze the audience with the following.

Suggest that you would like the audience to concentrate on the selected card. Say, "I want to get a burning impression of your selected card." Casually pull out your lighter and ignite it. Hold the business card just above the flame, placing the invisible message directly over the heat. Move the business card in a circular motion to keep it from catching on fire.

Figure 3

Eventually, the message will appear to be burnt into your business card, to everyone's amazement (FIG. 3). All you may hear is stunned silence. *Yet I promise that your audience will be impressed.* Rub off any black residue from the back of the business card as you give it to the spectator to keep.

Try other messages with Burning Impression. For example, the message "Happy Birthday" could appear on your business card. Perhaps you could predict a number someone is thinking of. You could predict the type of geometric shape an audience member chooses. Be creative!

The strength of the routine is that the effect is frozen in time. Every time the spectator looks at your business card, he or she will remember the effect—and you. I can't think of a better way to present a magician's business card. I hope you enjoy this reputation maker.

Trapdoor Coins

"There is a boundary to men's passions when they act from feelings; but none when they are under the influence of imagination."
Edmund Burke

<u>Effect</u>: Three half-dollars magically penetrate a table one at a time.

Required Items:
- ◆ Three half-dollar coins
- ◆ An opaque table to perform upon

Figure 1

The Routine:

I. First Penetration (The Transfer)

Begin by allowing the audience to examine the three half-dollars. As you take the coins back with your right hand, bounce them around until a coin lands in **Classic Palm** position (FIG. 1). Classic Palm one of the half-dollars as you turn the back of your right hand toward the audience. Let the other two coins fall to your right hand's fingertips while holding them in place with your thumb (FIG. 2). The audience will not be able to see exactly how many coins you are holding.

Figure 2

Toss the two halves into your left hand, closing the left hand into a relaxed fist. Concealing the palmed coin, place your right hand under the tabletop. Say, "Now to find the trapdoor in the table." Smash the two halves onto the tabletop with your left hand, palm down, with an open hand. Shortly thereafter, lift your left hand to reveal the two halves. Casually remove your right hand from under the table to reveal the coin. Upon seeing the coin in your right hand, the audience will be amazed. Place coin #1 into an empty pocket.

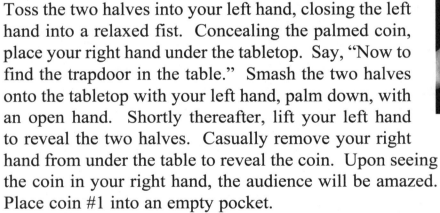

Figure 3

II. Second Penetration (Click Pass)

Pick up one of the two coins on the table with your right hand. Continuing with your right hand, execute the **Retention of Vision Vanish** (FIG. 3). As your right hand approaches the other coin on the table, Classic Palm the half that should be in **Finger Rest** position (FIG. 4). Pick up the tabled coin, placing it into Finger Rest position. With both halves now in position, execute the **Click Pass** (FIG. 5). With one half-dollar concealed in your right hand, place it under the tabletop.

Figure 4

Figure 5

All attention should be on your left hand, which is believed to be holding both coins. Once again, with your left hand, smash the half-dollar onto the tabletop. Lift your left hand for all to see that only one coin remains. Remove your right hand from under the tabletop to confirm the second penetration. Place coin #2 into your pocket with the first coin.

III. Final Penetration (Slydini's Convincer)

With your right hand, hold the last coin a couple of feet above the tabletop. Prepare to catch the coin with your left hand as you drop the coin with your right hand. Close your left hand into a loose fist around the coin and place your right hand under the tabletop. Smash the coin, as before, onto the tabletop. Acting somewhat disappointed, lift your left hand, revealing the half-dollar on the tabletop. Say, "I missed the trapdoor!"

Enacting this mistake makes you seem human. The subtlety takes the attention off your hands and allows the audience to let down its guard. In this moment you've created an advantage which you can use to execute the last sequence more discreetly.

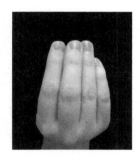

Figure 6

With your right hand, execute the Retention of Vision Vanish. Concealing the coin in your right hand, place it under the tabletop. Your left hand should mimic the grip of holding a coin at its fingertips (FIG. 6). With your left hand, pretend to tap the coin on the table while your right hand actually does so underneath the tabletop. This auditory illusion is called Slydini's Convincer.

With your left hand, appear to drag the coin a couple of inches across the tabletop while actually doing so underneath with your right hand. Finally, with your left hand's fingertips, pretend to push the coin through the table. Simultaneously, your right hand should push the coin flat against the underside of the table. Lift your left hand to reveal an empty hand. Slowly remove your right hand from under the table to reveal the final penetration.

Slydini was a legendary magician. Slydini's Convincer is only one of many clever additions he made to the art of close-up magic during his lifetime. When Slydini's Convincer is done correctly, the left hand mirrors the actions of the right hand. Practice the move until you can fool yourself with it.

The beauty of this routine is that it is immediately repeatable, and it can be performed sitting or standing. There are other coin-thru-table routines that use more intricate sleight of hand and/or gimmicks. With this effect you start clean and end clean. I live by the K.I.S.S. motto: Keep It Simple, Stupid.

Diamond Back

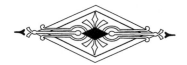

"MAGIC is real action. Something really happens, often something violent, usually something of consequence. People are shaken, influenced, healed, destroyed, transformed. The social situation is altered."
Daniel Lawerence O'Keefe
The Social Theory of Magic

<u>Effect</u>: The magician asks a spectator to select five cards from a pack. Each of the five cards has a letter of the alphabet printed on the back. Someone in the audience is instructed to make a word with the selected cards. After this has been done, the magician calls the audience's attention to a prediction that has been in plain view the whole time. Upon opening the prediction, the word is revealed and the audience receives a bonus surprise.

<u>Required Items:</u>
- ◆ A pencil
- ◆ A pair of scissors
- ◆ A pack of red-backed cards
- ◆ A black or blue permanent marker
- ◆ A thick piece of white posterboard
- ◆ A 5½- by 3-inch manila pay envelope, *preferably the kind with metal clasps used to keep it closed*
- ◆ A rattlesnake gimmick (FIG. 1). *This gimmick is packaged and sold for around a dollar in novelty stores as Rattlesnake Eggs.*

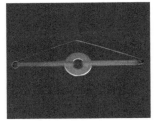

Figure 1

<u>Preparation:</u> Shuffle the pack of cards. Print a letter of the alphabet on the back of each of the playing cards with the permanent marker. Since there are twenty-six letters in the alphabet and fifty-two cards in the pack, you should mark two cards with each letter. Once all of the cards have been assigned a letter, shuffle them several times.

Remove the cards with the letters (A E K N S) from the pack. There should be a pair of cards for each letter. Separate the rest of the pack into two approximately equal halves and place them on the table face down next to one another. We will call the half on your left pile A and the half on your right pile B.

On top of pile A place each of the five letter cards in this order (N E K A S). On pile A the "S" should be the uppermost card showing (FIG. 2). On top of pile B place each of the remaining five letter cards in this order (S A K E N). On pile B the "N" should be the uppermost card showing (FIG. 2). Notice that the top five cards in the two piles are in reverse order.

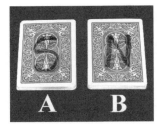

Figure 2

Remove the top cards (*letters S and N*) from pile A and B momentarily. Use your scissors to cut 1/16 of an inch off from the length of each of these cards. You have just created two **short cards**. On the back of each short card draw a pencil dot in the upper-left-hand and lower-right-hand corners (FIG. 3). Place the short cards back on top of their piles.

Figure 3

Place either pile on top of the other. Cut the pack, and then complete the cut until one of the special five letter cards (A E K N S) is not on top. Place the pack back into its box. The pack is now set.

Cut out a 2½ by 4½ inch rectangle from the posterboard. On one side print the word "SNEAK" in big bold letters. On the opposite side of the poster-board rectangle print the word "SNAKE" in big bold letters. This piece of posterboard will be referred to as your prediction card. Place it in the manila envelope.

Set the rattlesnake gimmick and carefully place it in the manila envelope. Close the flap of the manila envelope and put it into your jacket or shirt breast pocket. Place the prearranged deck in your pocket as well. Put on a straight face and you are ready to begin.

Presentation: Bring out the prepared pack and explain to your audience that you have printed a letter of the alphabet on each card. Hold the pack face down and spread the cards from hand to hand to show the backs of the cards (FIG. 4). Explain that you will have five cards selected and then put into an order of their choice to form a word in the English language. Further

Figure 4

explain that you have made a prediction of which word will be chosen as you place the manila envelope in plain view.

Give the pack a few **false shuffles** and/or cuts. This will make an impression on the audience a little later. Place the pack on the table and have your audience cut and complete the cut a few times. As you say, "Let's cut them once more," **riffle** the ends of the pack until you feel and hear it stop at one of the short cards. Separate the pack at this short card and cut it to the top of the pack. You can check the pencil dots on the back of the short card to be sure.

The pack should be face down on the table. Riffle and cut to the second short card and separate the face-down halves. Now each half has the special five cards on top. Turn each half face up and place them side by side. *I prefer that each half should be face up now so that no one gets a glimpse of the cards on top.* Have someone shuffle the two halves together just once.

Ask someone to turn the pack face down and remove the top five cards.

Although the cards have been mixed, you have just **forced** the spectator to select the five letter cards (A E K N S). You don't have to know exactly how this works, just that it does. Instruct the spectator to form a word using all five of the selected cards. Place the balance of the pack aside, face up, not calling attention to one of the five duplicate cards on top of the deck.

Figure 5

There are only two words in the English language that your audience can make with the five forced cards: SNEAK and SNAKE. If someone forms the word "SNEAK," then pick up your prediction and pinch the washer of the rattlesnake gimmick through the envelope. Carefully remove the prediction card, revealing the side with the word "SNEAK" (FIG. 5). The rattlesnake gimmick should not be set off.

Carefully place the prediction card back into the envelope. Obviously you should not reveal the word "SNAKE" prematurely. Take precautions not to set off the rattlesnake gimmick. Ask your audience if another word can be formed. Eventually, the audience will put together the word "SNAKE."

Say, "Now wouldn't you be surprised if you found a snake in the envelope?" Apprehensively, they will open the envelope and set off the rattlesnake gimmick. This will undoubtedly cause a surprised reaction from your audience. Once everyone has calmed down, remove the prediction card to reveal the side showing the word "SNAKE."

You will have no idea which of the two forced words will be selected first, but it doesn't matter. If a spectator forms the word "SNAKE" first, then permit the volunteer to open the envelope and set off the rattlesnake gimmick. Reveal the prediction card with the correct side showing. As an afterthought, if someone asks, "What if we had chosen the word *sneak*?" reply, "A good magician is always prepared," as you flip over the prediction card to reveal the word "SNEAK."

Alternate "Scary" Ending Preparation: Make up another manila envelope with the word *prediction* printed on the front of it. Cut open the bottom of the manila envelope. Take a long rubber snake and place it down the front of your pants (FIG. 6). Make sure the head of the snake sticks out of the waistband of your pants. The head of the snake

Figure 6

should be pulled over to your left side to rest against your hip. Your jacket will hide the snake's presence from the audience.

Alternate "Scary" Ending Performance: As you are gathering the items used in the Diamond Back routine to place them in your pockets, slyly remove the bottomless **gaffed** manila envelope and place it on the table. The audience should be completely relaxed at this moment. Say, "Wouldn't you have been surprised if I had really pulled a snake from the envelope?" They'll be thinking, "Yeah, right!"

As you reach for the envelope with your right hand, your left hand should catch the rubber snake's head between the crotch of your index finger and thumb (FIG. 7). Pull the snake towards your navel and allow your left hand to remain still. Your right hand should squeeze open the envelope and place it in your left hand, while you are covering the snake's head with the cut-open end of the envelope. Reach into the envelope with your right hand to get a good pinched-grip on the snake's head (FIG. 8).

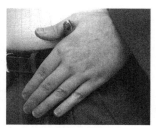

Figure 7

Figure 8

Yank the snake free from the envelope and your pants. The illusion of pulling a long snake from a small envelope is amusing in and of itself. Needless to say, the terror of producing a snake will make some of your audience members climb the walls. *Usually, I'll throw the snake on the person who seems to be screaming the loudest. I'm kidding, of course.* Use good judgement when producing the snake, because you have just done something that your audience will probably never forget.

Perform this routine for little kids, the elderly, pregnant women, or people with food in their mouths. Obviously I'm joking! I cannot tell you the best time and place to perform the Diamond Back routine. Only your own experience will dictate that for you.

*This **mentalism** routine is sure to cause your audience's hair to stand up, whether you produce the rubber snake or not. It's fun to have a good harmless scare every now and then. The Diamond Back routine, when used* *properly, should capture your audience's undivided attention for the rest of your performance. Do not use the routine to make the audience afraid or to distrust you.*

Reel Fun

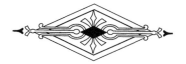

"Everybody likes a kidder, but nobody lends him money."
Arthur Miller

<u>Effect</u>: A dollar bill, which is several feet from the magician, magically leaps from the floor into the magician's pocket.

Required Items:
- ◆ A safety pin
- ◆ A hand-held Mini-Fan (FIG. 1)
- ◆ Some invisible or Scotch® tape and a dollar bill
- ◆ A bobbin *the size of an American quarter* (FIG. 2)
- ◆ A spool of clear monofilament, *known in fabric stores as Invisible Thread* (FIG. 3)

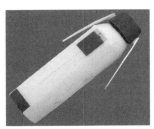

Figure 1

Many readers may be familiar with the novelty item referred to as a Dollar Snatcher. If not, envision a reel with a dollar attached to the line that snaps back to you at will. *I've always enjoyed the concept of the Dollar Snatcher, but the line on the gimmick is usually too short.* And when Dollar Snatchers break, they are next to impossible to repair.

Figure 2

Recently, the magic community has seen many new motorized reels on the market. These reels have longer lines and are easier to repair. Yet they cost $40 or more. My homemade reel will cost you in the neighborhood of $5 to make. My reel works as well as, or better than, others on the market.

Figure 3

Preparation: First, take the head (the fan blades) off the Mini-Fan. Tie the Invisible Thread to the center of the bobbin. Make several knots. Wind the desired length of thread around the bobbin. *I prefer to fill half of the bobbin's capacity or less.*

Figure 4

Place the bobbin onto the Mini-Fan in place of the fan blades. It should be a snug fit. Now either glue or tape the safety pin onto the fan, as shown in FIG. 4. Run the loose end of the thread through the hole in the end of the safety pin. Attach the loose end of the thread to the dollar bill with tape (FIG. 5). Now you are ready for the fun!

Figure 5

<u>Hook, Line and Sinker</u>: Stretch the length of the thread out from the reel about 15 to 25 feet away from where you are standing. Make sure there is a clear path between you and the dollar bill. Test it by flipping the switch of the fan to ON. The dollar bill should zip back to you. Assuming it does so, immediately turn the fan back to OFF once the dollar has returned.

The fan can be hidden in your hands or, better yet, in your pants pocket. When you turn the fan ON, be sure to turn it OFF the second that the dollar retracts to you. If you leave the fan ON too long, two things could happen. (1) The thread could break, or (2) eventually the motor of the fan will burn out.

Once you have tested the motorized reel, try it in a large crowded place. This is very similar to fishing. If you have patience, someone will eventually bite. *Sometimes I'll allow "the fish" to pick up the bill, only to have it yanked from his or her hand. Or sometimes, once the person bends down, I'll hit the ON switch and then immediately hit OFF. This ON-OFF action causes the dollar to scoot across the floor a short distance as if the wind had lifted it momentarily. Repeat this action until "the fish" figures out that it's been caught.*

<u>Maintenance</u>:
If the motorized reel seems to be having problems, then check the following:
◆ The batteries might need to be replaced.
◆ Sometimes the thread gets wrapped around the underside of the bobbin and the motor's stem. If so, cut the thread free and redo the hook-up.
◆ If the thread gets tangled in knots, cut it free and rethread the bobbin.
◆ If the thread bobbin seems loose, remove it and place a small piece of cellophane onto the motor's stem. Force the bobbin down onto the motor, and it should remain snug.
◆ If, after several uses, the fan doesn't seem to work properly, then buy another one. The fan will cost a couple of bucks.

Use your imagination when thinking of applications for the motorized reel. I've used it in the play Dracula *to make a bat fly across the length of a stage. I've used it in a* **Change Bag** *routine, in which a scarf on the floor is made to jump back into the bag. During a* **seance**, *it could be used to make an item fall from a table or shelf. The possibilities are endless.*

Have fun with this clever novelty item. Do not attach to the reel more money than you can afford to lose. Sometimes the line will break. Sometimes the thread pulls free from the tape on the dollar. Anytime you're pulling a trick on someone, do not forget: There is always someone out there who is more clever than you are!

Frog Hair

"I see nobody on the road," said Alice.
"I only wish I had such eyes," the King remarked in a fretful tone. "To be able to see Nobody! And at that distance too! Why, it's as much as I can do to see real people, by this light!"
Lewis Carroll
Through the Looking-Glass

<u>Effect</u>: The magician displays a *frog hair*, which to the audience seems invisible. The magician ties the hair to a playing card and lays the card flat in his left hand. Shockingly, as he pulls the *frog hair* from the opposite end, the card stands up and flips over in his hand. The card is passed out to the audience for examination.

Method: Sorry, no invisible threads are used here. This is a genuine sleight-of-hand trick. Your left hand does the dirty work while your right hand misdirects the audience. Secretly, your left hand *scrunches* its outstretched fingers inward toward your palm. This action will make the card flip over if the card is positioned in the hand correctly; *I will refer to this action as the Scrunch Move.*

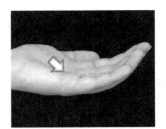

Figure 1

Scrunch Move: Place one of the corners of the card into the natural bend in the hand, just below your pinkie finger (FIGS. 1 & 2). Keep the fingers of your left hand straight; move them inward slightly, and the groove in your hand will grab the card. If you continue to pull your fingers inward, the middle of your left hand will bend downward. This action will bring the fleshy padded area beside the base of your thumb upward. Believe it or not, the momentum from this action will cause the card to stand up (FIG. 3). Once the card is vertical, give it a little kick, with the same squeezing motion, and allow the card to topple over (FIG. 4).

Figure 2

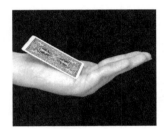

Figure 3

Pointers: The Scrunch Move should be done in one fluid motion rather than as a series of movements. The left hand should appear flat before and after the card flips completely over. As you execute the Scrunch Move, keep your left fingers straight as you bend them upward. Do not curl your fingers. Remember that this should be done with the audience looking down at the card so that, as you execute the Scrunch Move, the hand appears flat.

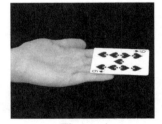

Figure 4

Presentation: First, introduce the *frog hair* by removing it from your pocket. The audience should comment, "Frogs don't have any hair!" Yet you insist they do, but you add, "You just can't see it; it's invisible." Proclaim this to be one of the magician's best-kept secrets and that it is used to accomplish many effects.

Demonstrating the hair's usefulness, pretend to attach it to a playing card by wrapping the hair around it, tying a knot. Place the card into your left hand, positioning it correctly, as shown in FIG. 2. As you do this, pretend to be holding on to the opposite end of the hair with your right hand. Now pretend to pull the card to a standing position and then flip it over, executing the Scrunch Move (FIGS. 3 & 4).

Act as if you are breaking the hair free by pinching the card where the knot is supposed to be. As you do this, bow the card slightly and quickly pull the pinching fingers away, creating a snapping or popping sound (FIG. 5). This action gives the auditory illusion of the hair being broken free from the card. Finish by handing an audience member the card to examine, and give someone the *frog hair* to keep as a souvenir.

Figure 5

The Scrunch Move is not one that you will perfect overnight. Your actions must appear effortless when making the card flip over. Your left hand should appear absolutely still during the routine. After performing the effect, your audience should be convinced there is a possibility that frog hair actually exists.

*Once you have perfected the Scrunch Move, you will have lots of fun with it. Frog Hair is a trick you can do almost anytime and anywhere. I'm sure that you will want to try it with a business card, and it will work. Remember that a playing card fills more space in the hand and demands the attention of your audience. Whereas a small business card allows the audience to view more of the hand, which makes the Scrunch Move difficult to execute discreetly. Practice the move by bending the hand at first, and try it with different types of cards. When performing the effect, I recommend using a **Poker-size** playing card.*

Sacring of Wicca

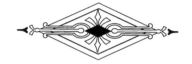

"O, Faustus, lay that damned book aside,
and gaze not on it, lest it tempt thy soul."
Christopher Marlowe
The Tragical History of Dr. Faustus

<u>Effect</u>: A card from a tarot pack is selected. The card's identity is written on a piece of paper. The paper is set aflame, destroying any evidence of the selection. The remaining ash is rubbed on the magician's forearm. Magically, the ash spells out the name of the selection.

Required Items:

◆ An ashtray
◆ A moist towel
◆ A cotton swab
◆ A pen or pencil
◆ Lemon juice or soap
◆ A pack of tarot cards
◆ A small tablet of paper
◆ A pack of matches or a lighter

Preparation: Use a **tarot** pack for the element of mystery. Any **force** may be used, but I prefer the **Reversed Card Force** for this effect. Place the **force card** (ex: *The Fool*) into position. Before presenting the effect, simply write the word "FOOL" on your left forearm with a cotton-swab dipped in lemon juice or wet soap. Once this is done, let it dry well on your arm. During the presentation, have your arm prepared. Gather your props and you are ready to begin.

Presentation: First, tell a good spooky story to set the stage. Next, force the desired card. Have the spectator write the card's identity on the piece of paper. Have him burn the paper. Rub the ash on the prepared area of your arm. Amazingly, the ash clings to the invisible message on your arm, making it visible for all to see. Keep a glass of water and a towel handy to wash the message off. Don't wash the message away too soon. It is a very magical moment when the card's identity is revealed on your arm in ashes!

The ashes-on-the-arm bit has always been a favorite of mine. The following story helps to set the mood for this hair-raising effect. The story provided may be long-winded, but it captures the essence of the effect. The story also explains why someone might do such a strange thing and how he might have learned it. Please read the story, embellish it, and make it your own!

Just one more sucker—excuse me, customer—and then I'd call it a night. Selling vacuum cleaners, pots and pans, and encyclopedias from door to door was one thing. But traveling the back roads of the southern United States was another. Twilight was fast approaching, and the road I was on didn't show up on any of the maps that I had in the glove box of my '69 Camaro. It had just begun to rain, and the dread of spending the evening in a bar ditch swatting flies and scratching bites vanished as I caught the twinkle of a porchlight out of the corner of my eye.

"Well, maybe this customer would provide my dinner for the night," I mused. Slowly lurching up the pebble driveway, my car stalled and stopped in its tracks. My Camaro seemed afraid to get any closer to the structure we were approaching. The house was extremely unattractive. It looked as though someone had haphazardly nailed one board onto another to hide the house's contents. Grabbing my sales material, I followed my nose to the front door, where I could smell some most unusual and interesting aromas.

As I started to knock on the ajar door, I heard an elderly women scream, "Bast! Bast! Bast!" Panicked, I looked down and saw what I thought was a black cat dart between my legs from inside the dwelling. I remember thinking that this was not a good omen. Still screaming, an old woman flung open the door and froze in mid-step upon seeing me. Collecting herself, she said, "Hello, please come in; I've been expecting you." Entering her home, I heard her scream again, "Bad kitty!"

As I followed the gray-haired woman to her dining room table, she began lighting several candles until the room was aglow. A quick glance around the room revealed a flea market of oddities, from bottles filled with colorful liquids to shiny etched stones lying on shelves. As I turned toward the short stocky woman, she instructed me, "Please sit, and I will answer all your questions!" She then bobbled her way to a bookshelf to fetch an odd-looking package.

Preparing my sales spiel, I exclaimed, "A lovely home like this would be even nicer with a Zoom-A-Matic. . . ." She interrupted, "Shh! Shh! First, before I tell your future, we must make a *sacring of wicca*." Confused, I replied, "Excuse me?" My confusion inspired her to respond sternly, "An appeasement to the spirits." "Oh!" I complied, as she began to chant in a foreign tongue. With each syllable she spoke, I assured myself that this was not going to be an easy sale. Disgusted, I had decided to mark her off as a losing proposition. After she finished the chant, she placed her mysterious package on the table. She began delicately unfolding a red silk scarf. Inside the scarf was a deck of cards, tarot cards.

As I curiously awaited her next move, she demanded that I place the pack underneath the table, hiding the cards from her view. "Select one," she snickered, "and turn your future face up on top of the pack!" I did so. "Now," she said, smiling with her remaining teeth, "cut it into the center of the pack." Once again I obeyed her. "Don't worry. All your questions will be answered shortly," she said as she pulled a piece of paper from her pocket. Unfortunately, though, I was worried, as she could see by watching the sweat drip from my brow.

She produced a feather from a drawer in her table and dipped the quill into a nearby vial. The vial appeared to be full of blood, yet I prayed that it was red ink. She then barked, "Look at what you have chosen, and write!" Following her instructions, I thumbed through the cards quickly. Shocked, I discovered that I had selected a card marked "The Sacrifice."

Once I had scribbled the word upon the strangely decorated paper, I folded it, clenching it in my fist away from her piercing eyes. Laughingly she muttered, "Burn it!" I complied by placing it into the nearest candle flame. Dropping the ball of fire onto the table, I watched it until it extinguished itself. With the speed of a snake attacking its prey, she snatched the paper, now transformed into ash. As I sat with my mouth agape, she began to rub the filth on her forearm.

While I watched this ritual, the strangest breeze came over us. I remember hearing thunder in the distance and feeling the rain that trickled in through her leaky roof. Bizarrely, the ash that she had rubbed on her arm began to form letters, letters that seemed to form a word, the word on my card, the word *sacrifice*!

Utterly confused by what had happened, I looked into her hypnotic eyes. Transfixed, her glare seemed to suck the soul out of my body. Slowly she shook her head yes and grunted, "You are the chosen one." Afraid of what that meant, I objected, "No. I am not the one, and I think I had better leave now!" She placed her quill back into the drawer and slyly produced a dagger. She snarled, "Come here, my child."

I recall thinking, "This lady definitely doesn't want a vacuum cleaner." I deduced that I should find the closest exit. As I leaped to my feet, I flipped the immense table upon her. Reacting, she began hissing and screaming curses and my name. During the pandemonium, shelves and candles began tumbling over. Soon thereafter, the sounds of breaking glass and rippling flames engulfed the room. Wanting to correct what I had done, I grabbed what I thought was my sales book and began trying to pat out the fire. Unfortunately, the flames had consumed most of the room. I will never forget how the woman, witch, or whatever she was kept threatening to kill me as the fire swept all around us.

Delirious, I fled toward the door, only to discover that it had been locked with a key. The key was missing. Terrified, I ran to the nearest window, only to behold that it had been nailed shut. Frantic, I paced her den, searching for something substantial enough to break the window. All the while I listened to the moans and groans of the burning witch. Suddenly I noticed a large Egyptian statue of some dog-like god, and I lifted it up and over my shoulder. Heaving it toward the window, I watched my glass reflection shatter before me. Barely ahead of the fire, I jumped to safety and landed on the porch.

Free from the inferno, I ran in the rain to my car as I fumbled for my keys. Occasionally I looked back over my shoulder, hoping that the witch was still pinned under the table. Victoriously I opened my car door and hopped inside. Realizing that I still had the book under my arm, I tossed it into the passenger seat. Thankfully my car started on the first crank, and I punched the gas. I threw the car into drive. Its tires hurled pebbles, flinging them toward the house. Finally, gripping the moist terrain, I got traction and sped off.

I traveled down many dark roads that night while trying to recall all that had taken place. I prayed, without a guilty conscience, that the storm had not extinguished the fire. Not until I made it to my motel room, some two hours later, did I discover what I had come to possess. The book in the seat next to me was titled *Sacring of Wicca*. Although I was afraid to open these god-forbidden pages, I did so anyway. Surprised, I discovered several of the witch's age-old secrets.

Now that several years have passed since this event, I am free to tell my story. Since no one can prove whether what I have written is fact or fiction, I feel at ease with this confession. For the last eight years now, I, a master Wiccan, have been making a comfortable living as a sage of sorts. The book contains several spells and secrets that could easily alter any man's destiny.

Ironically, I credit my awakening to the old hag who passed the book on to me in such a roundabout way. Looking back, I realize that it was a magical night for the witch and me. She said there would be a sacrifice that night. I guess it was in the cards. Little did she know that she would be predicting her own death. Spooky, huh?

There is an old saying that the best place to hide a secret is in a book. I write this laughingly, knowing that I have THE BOOK.

◆ ◆ ◆

The Smoking Spoon

"Not he is great who can alter matter,
but he who can alter my state of mind."
Ralph Waldo Emerson
The American Scholar

<u>Effect</u>: The magician gives a demonstration of mind over matter. Borrowing a spoon, he begins to rub the neck of the spoon. The audience sees the spoon bend while smoke trails from the area being rubbed. When the magician finishes, the contorted spoon and magician's hands can be examined. The audience is completely spooked.

<u>Required Items:</u>
- ◆ Some Magic Smoke
- ◆ A couple of cheap-quality metal spoons

Magic Smoke can be found in most novelty stores. It is a sticky substance that, when rubbed between one's fingers, creates the illusion of smoke. *However, I do not prefer the store brand of Magic Smoke. Typically, the store brand looks stringy and is too sticky to work with. I prefer to make my own Magic Smoke.*

<u>How to make Magic Smoke:</u> Cut the striking surface from a box or book of matches. Remove as much of the paper from it as you can. Set the striking surface on fire. Place the striking surface, brown side down, while it's still burning, into a glass receptacle such as an ashtray.

Once the striking surface has completely burned, remove the paper ash, and a brown residue will remain. The brown residue is the Magic Smoke. Some striking surfaces work better than others. *I've found that the darker the brown surface is, the better it works to create the Magic Smoke.*

 Note that the Magic Smoke residue is toxic. Do not get the residue in your mouth or eyes. The substance has a high red phosphorus content. Do not inhale the smoke when you burn the striking surface. First of all, it stinks, and second, it's probably not good for you.

Touch your right hand's middle finger to the brown residue. Rub the small amount that adheres to your finger vigorously against your right hand's thumb. Continue to rub your middle finger and thumb back and forth to watch the magic happen. You will see and smell smoke coming from your fingers.

Since the residue is toxic and sticky, wash your hands afterwards. When you sit down to create the Magic Smoke, make a substantial amount. Preserve the residue in an air-tight container for later use.

Routine: Have the Magic Smoke easily accessible or have some concealed on your right hand's middle finger ready to use. Borrow a couple of spoons, or have some handy, and have them examined. Tell any of your favorite psychic stories. You could refer to Uri Geller, Edgar Cayce, etc. Perhaps you could refer to the use of psychics by the police to help solve crimes.

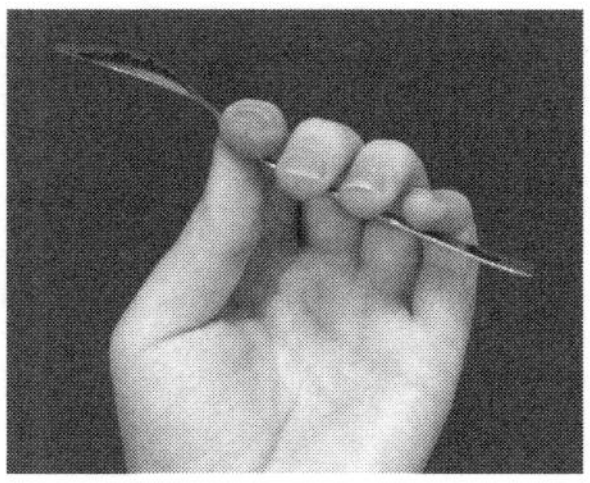

Figure 1

Tell a story by leading into the ability psychics have to move or even bend objects with the power of their minds. Demonstrating your point, hand one of the two spoons to someone. Say, "We all have psychic powers. We must learn how to exercise our minds to use them." Take the other spoon in your left hand and hold it as shown in FIG. 1.

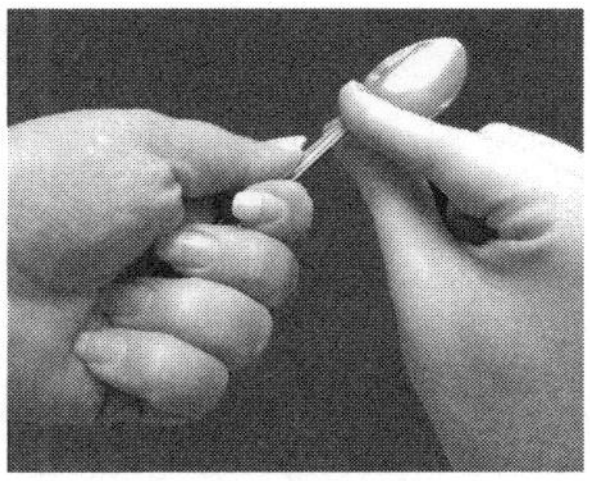

Figure 2

Position the spoon in your left hand about chest high for all to see. State, "Psychic powers can be used to do the strangest things!" as you look at your spoon. Directing attention toward the spectator, say, "Concentrate your energy on the spoon and rub it like this." Grip the spectator's spoon at the neck with the index finger and thumb of your right hand. Mimic the action of rubbing the spoon with the same fingers (FIG. 2). Be careful not to expose the residue on your right hand's middle finger.

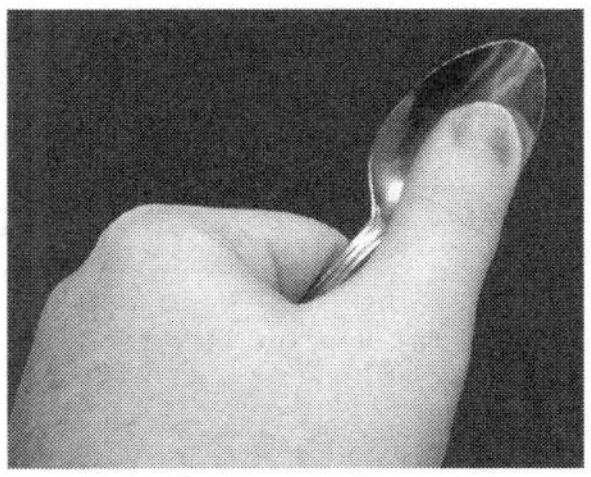

Figure 3

Giving this direct command will force everyone's attention on the spoon in the participant's hand. During this brief moment, let your left arm relax at your side, keeping the spoon in your hand. Gripping the spoon firmly, place your left hand's thumb on the bowl of the spoon (FIG. 3). Bend the head of the spoon back using your left hand's thumb (FIG. 4). Regrip the spoon, concealing the bend in it (FIG. 5).

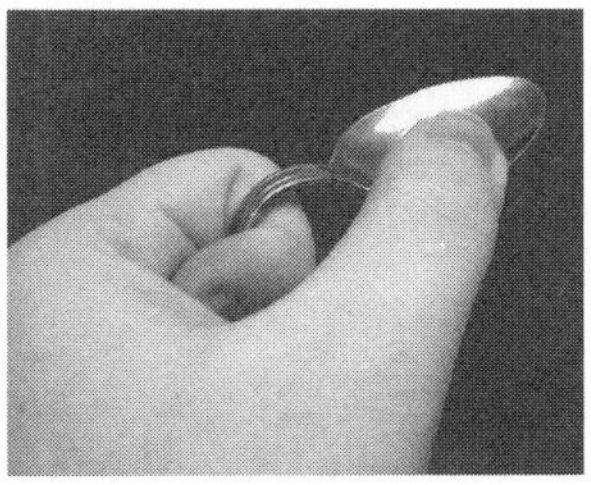

Figure 4

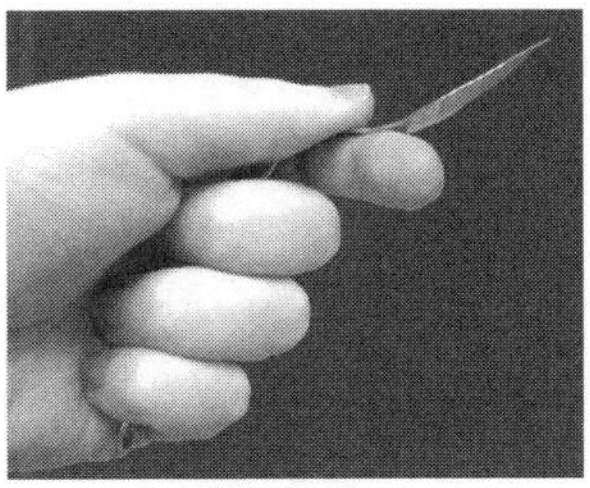

Figure 5

If the spoon does not bend easily, it may be made of steel. In this case, use your leg as a wedge to help bend the spoon.

Calling attention to your spoon, raise it chest high again. Rub the spoon on its neck with your right hand's index finger, middle finger and thumb. As your fingers rub the spoon, everyone will start to see smoke. Grit your teeth and act as if you are willing the spoon to bend. The audience will be awe-struck.

Slowly, centimeter by centimeter, push the spoon from your left hand while rubbing it with your right hand's fingers. This pushing and rubbing action creates the illusion of the spoon bending before the audience's eyes. After about a minute of this, hand the spoon out for all to see. Gesture nonchalantly with your hands, being careful not to expose any residue that might remain on your fingertips.

Wrapping things up, you jest, "Yes, there is a higher power. But I am just a servant, merely a tool." *Some magicians may scoff at my use of humor at the end of this effect. Some believe that such a mysterious and bizarre effect should not be trivialized with comedy. However, I don't want the audience thinking that I am Satan in disguise.* The joke lets the audience know that you do not take yourself too seriously.

Take into consideration, when you bend someone's silverware, it never seems to straighten back to its normal self. Besides creating streams of smoke, the toxic Magic Smoke residue has other unique properties. After the residue is held to the light, it glows in the dark. If you would like to learn another handling for The Smoking Spoon, and another effect using Magic Smoke, see Michael Weber's book Life Savers. *For a somewhat darker routine, read Tony Andruzzi's original idea with Magic Smoke called The Witches Nail in* The New Invocation *magazine, which was recently reprinted in the book* The Compleat Invocation.

Diamond's Dazzler

"If the creator had a purpose in equipping us with a neck,
he surely meant us to stick it out."
Arthur Koestler
Encounter

<u>Effect</u>: A selected card magically leaps out from the middle of the deck, face up, onto the table.

<u>Preparation</u>: To execute Diamond's Dazzler, you must place the chosen card on the face of the pack. Begin by **controlling** a selected card to the bottom of the deck. *I prefer using the **Kelly Bottom Placement (K.B.P.)**.* It is crucial to learn the K.B.P., since the position of your hands during Diamond's Dazzler is similar. Study and perfect the K.B.P. before reading any further.

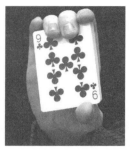

Figure 1

<u>Executing Diamond's Dazzler</u>: Use your right hand to grasp the deck from above. Position your right hand's fingers, as shown in FIG. 1. The middle and ring finger of your right hand should press firmly against the underside of the deck. Your right hand's remaining fingers are used to keep the pack square.

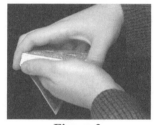

Figure 2

The tips of your right middle and ring fingers should exert slight pressure on the selected card. These fingers should pull the selected card slightly up and over the front edge of the deck. This action will free the selection from the grip of your right thumb and the face of the deck, creating a V-shaped angle between the selection and the face of the pack (FIG. 2). Do not make this angle too wide. This action is masked from the audience by your right hand and the angle at which the cards are held.

Figure 3

Angle the front edge of the deck toward the floor as your left hand approaches the pack from underneath. Slide your left hand into the V-shaped opening created by your right hand (FIG. 3). Your left thumb rests against the length of the deck, near the corner, next to your right index finger. Your left hand's remaining fingers cradle the opposite side of the pack.

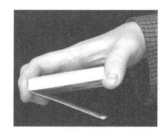

Figure 4

Using your right hand's index finger, lift about half of the cards approximately an inch (FIG. 4). Using your right middle and ring finger, pull the bottom card of the deck up and over the edge of the lower half of the pack. Keep pulling the selection until it rotates itself face up between the halves of the deck (FIG. 5).

Figure 5

This action should be done swiftly. Releasing the selection from the tips of your right middle and ring fingers will cause the card to look as if it is flying from the middle of the deck. To strengthen the appearance of this illusion, separate the halves in each hand about a foot as the card leaps face up onto the table (FIG. 6). Your audience is sure to be amazed!

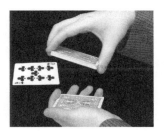

Figure 6

If you are a serious student of card magic, then you will notice many similarities between Diamond's Dazzler and J. K. Hartman's Pop-Out Move. I have never seen anyone use Hartman's move to convince an audience that the card flips over magically. Rather, the move is used as a display of skill to reverse a card quickly. My modification takes Hartman's work a step further by making the selection magically fly face up from the center of the pack.

*Practice this finger-flinging maneuver until you have it perfected. Instead of using Diamond's Dazzler as a short routine, make it part of one of your favorite card routines. Perhaps you could use it in a **Four-Ace routine** to reveal the last Ace. I developed this maneuver to add pizzazz to the world of card artistry, not to stand alone.*

Nimble Corks

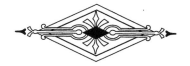

*"If at first you don't succeed, try, try again.
Then quit. No use being a damn fool about it."*
W.C. Fields
Quoted in John Robert Colombo's *Popcorn in Paradise*

Effect: A challenge is made with two large corks. The challenge is to simultaneously flip the corks over together three times. This feat is difficult to perform, since the participant can use only the index and middle finger of one hand. However, the magician can successfully complete the challenge each time. When volunteers attempt the challenge, the corks shoot from between their fingers.

Required Items:

♦Two large corks approximately an inch in length and an inch in diameter across the head of the cork. *It is best to use tapered beaker corks rather than wine bottle corks.*

This was one of my friend Lew Zafran's favorite bits. It is an old party stunt that could be used as a bar bet if so desired. I prefer, as Lew did, to use it as a challenge to those in an intimate gathering. I like to tell my audience that "this is an agility test given to amateur magicians before they are accepted into the brotherhood."

Rules:

♦ The corks should not be near the edge of the table.

♦ The corks must be facing the same direction.

♦ The participant can use only the index and middle finger of one hand.

♦ The corks must be touching, side by side, when turning them over.

♦ Each finger can touch only one of the corks, as shown in FIG. 1, as opposed to having both corks touching both fingers, as shown in FIG. 2.

♦ If either of the corks falls over before the third attempt is completed, then the participant must start over.

♦ The corks must be turned over with the hand palm down. *Not really, but that's what you should tell your audience for now.*

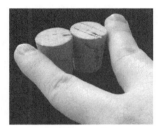

Figure 1

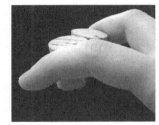

Figure 2

Figure 3

Secret: When explaining how to execute this trick, extend your fingers straight (FIG. 1). When performing the challenge, grip the corks between your index and middle fingers (like scissors), but then slightly bend your fingers toward your palm (FIG. 3). Turn the corks over quickly and surreptitiously straighten your fingers after doing so. Repeat the effect twice more.

Routine: A spectator tries it unsuccessfully. You accomplish it. Another spectator tries it. You do it again. Let someone else try it. Do this a few times and move on to something else. *If your audience is able to accomplish it, you have not failed. In fact, by solving the mystery, the spectator will feel the sense of pride that a master magician has. Either way, you have entertained your audience.*

The great thing about the Nimble Corks routine is that kids enjoy trying it as much as adults do. If you want members of the audience to figure it out, then let them have as many tries as it may take. They will eventually get the hang of it. After spectators think they've mastered the technique, tell them to try it palm up. They will have some problems trying it this way, and so will you unless you've practiced. So get busy. Find two large beaker corks, start practicing, and I promise this will soon become one of your favorite bits of business.

*If you enjoy performing **impromptu** tricks with simple objects, then by all means seek and find the* Encyclopedia of Impromptu Magic *by Martin Gardner.*

Wise Guys Can't Count

"Ay, sir; to be honest, as this world goes,
is to be one man picked out of ten thousand."
Shakespeare
Hamlet

Effect: A wise guy is asked to count from 10 to 1 backward without screwing up. He can't do it.

*If you enjoyed the Three Burnt Matches routine, then you'll love this. This is another **con** that can be used as the equalizer between you and a wise guy. Once you have been "taken for a ride," try the following routine to even the score.*

10
9
8
7
6
5
4
3
2
1

<u>Routine</u>: Ask the wise guy to put up some money for a simple test. Once the wager is on the table, say, "I want you to try to count from 10 to 1 backward without screwing up." Tell him that if he screws up, then you get to keep the money on the table. Pretend to hypnotize him and say, "Go ahead and try it."

Being careful, he will count in a loud clear voice, "10, 9, 8, 7, 6, 5, 4, 3, 2, 1." Thinking he has succeeded, he will relax and smile.

Pick up the money and put it in your pocket, saying, "Sorry, you screwed up." Confused and indignant, he will say, "What?" Explain, "Correctly counting from 10 to 1, backwards, would be 1, 2, 3, 4, 5, 6, 7, 8, 9, 10." Tricked, he will not be able to deny your explanation.

If you work in restaurants and bars, then you know about wise guys. Wise guys want you to buy them a drink or pay for their dinner if you cannot perform a simple task. The simple task is usually a trick or a con of some sort. This is why you should never play the con man's game, unless you are prepared to lose. If you insist on playing, at least now you have some ammunition against these guys.

If you would like to learn more practical bar bets or impromptu bits of business, then look for my book series: Bamboozlers—The Book of Bankable Bar Betchas, Brain Bogglers, Belly Busters & Bewitchery.

Whatever It Takes

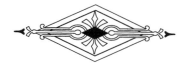

*"When you have eliminated the impossible,
whatever remains, however improbable, must be the truth."*
Sir Arthur Conan Doyle
Sign of Four

<u>Effect</u>: A number, letter, and card are selected by audience members and revealed by the magician in a comical and mystical manner.

In October 1995, Bill Goldman published his first in a series of articles entitled "Bill Goldman's Magic Bar and Grill." Each of these articles is about six pages long and packed full of good, solid working material. The first issue included an effect titled "Whatever," which accomplished the same effect as described here. However, the effect did not fit into a jacket pocket or reset as quickly as my own adaptation of it. I refined the handling, keeping the effect's strong points intact, and created a sure-fire stunner for the walk-around magician. After reading this, I think that Mr. Goldman would agree that I have taken a different road altogether to get to the same end.

Required Items:
◆A pen
◆At least six of your own business cards
◆A small knife or razor blade. *I use an Exacto® knife.*
◆A pack of high-quality cards *such as* **Poker Bicycle**®, *with their box*
◆A square pack of Post-It Notes® (3" x 3"), *preferably a dark color such as red, orange or blue.*

Figure 1

Preparation: (The Gaffed Cardbox)
Remove the cards from their box and set them aside. You are going to cut a slit into the back of the cardbox (the side with the back of a card printed on it). Using the razor blade or knife, cut the slit half an inch from the bottom of the box. The slit should run the length of the printed card design and stop at the white border (FIG. 1). Cut only one layer of the cardbox.

Figure 2

Now you are going to make another slit. Cut the next slit $1/16$ inch above the first slit and exactly the same length. Join the two slits by cutting the ends of the strip you've made. Discard this piece, creating a small window in the cardbox (FIG. 2). Place the Seven of Diamonds into **force** position and put all of the cards back into the box.

Figure 3

On the back of several of your business cards, draw a stick figure as I have done in FIG. 3. The reason for the boxes and position of the stick figure on the business card will become apparent shortly. The **force card**, drawn in the center box, could obviously be replaced with the card of your choice. Place one of the prepared business cards into the cardbox's slit as far as it will go. Be sure that the stick figure is upright and facing outward (FIG. 3).

Remove three Post-It Notes from their pack. On the first Post-It Note write the abbreviation of your force card (ex: 7D or 7♦). *Use the same pen type and color when preparing and performing the effect, for the sake of continuity.* Place the "7♦ Post-It Note" behind the business card protruding from the slit in the cardbox (FIG. 4). The top sticky edge of this Post-It Note should be stuck to the cardbox, closest to the end that opens. The bottom edge of the Post-It Note, which bears the name of the force card, should be as close to the slit as possible (FIG. 5).

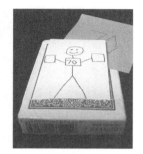

Figure 4

The remaining two blank Post-It Notes should be placed on top of the business card protruding from the slit in the cardbox. These two blank Post-It Notes should be squared with the Post-It Note behind the business card (FIG. 6). Of course you should press the Post-It Notes down to adhere them. It should appear that you have a few Post-It Notes stuck to the back of a cardbox. Place the prepared pack and the same pen into your jacket pocket, and you will be ready to blow your spectators' minds.

Figure 5

Figure 6

Routine: Remove the prepared pack from your pocket. Place the pack on the table, with the Post-It Notes' side showing. This visually reinforces the fact that the Post-It Notes are blank. Explain that you will have three people think of three different items. Further explain that you have already made a prediction about these items.

Ask a spectator to name a letter of the alphabet aloud. Let's assume that he or she says "J." Write the letter "J" on the outermost Post-It Note, large enough for all to see. Have someone close hold up his or her right hand. Peel off and adhere the "J Post-It Note" to the volunteer's right hand.

After peeling off the first Post-It Note, hold the prepared pack close to your body about chest high. The side of the pack with the Post-It Notes should be facing you. With only one Post-It Note covering the business card, there is a chance that your secret stick figure might become visible to the audience. After removing the next Post-It Note, the business card will not be covered at all, so watch your angles.

Next, ask someone different to name aloud a number between one and one hundred. Let's assume that he or she says "44." Write the number "44" on the outermost Post-It Note. Now have your human message board hold up his or her left hand. Peel off and adhere the "44 Post-it Note" to your volunteer's left hand.

Remove the playing cards from their box. Be careful not to expose the business card protruding from the slit in the cardbox. Place the cardbox on the table, business card side down, and act as if the box is unimportant. Force the Seven of Diamonds on a different spectator and have him show the card to the rest of the audience. Place the cards aside, but not in their box. Ask this spectator, "What card are you thinking of?" The spectator will respond with the name of the force card.

Notice the previous question's particular wording. Since the letter "J" and number "44" were thought of, it is important that the audience believes that the card could have been thought of as well. If you imply that the card was thought of, then likely your audience will remember it this way. You would be amazed what people will remember and how they might embellish an effect when telling a friend about it.

Figure 7

Once the spectator responds with the name of the force card, pick up the pack with the business card facing you. Write the letter "J" in the box to the left of the stick figure. Write the number "44" in the box to the right of the stick figure. Your audience will assume that you are writing the name of the card on the last Post-It Note (FIG. 7).

With whichever hand you are using to hold the cardbox chest high, gently use its thumb to press the business card against the back side of the box. Use your other hand to peel off the last Post-It Note, with the Seven of Diamonds abbreviated on it, and pull it free from the cardbox. The audience should not suspect anything. Look at your Post-It Note pal, with his or her hands in the air, and act as if you don't know where to adhere the last Post-It Note. Stick the "7♦ Post-It Note" just under your pal's neck on his or her chest.

Recap for the audience all that has been "freely chosen" as you prepare for the last bit of business. You must now convincingly remove the business card from inside the cardbox. There are two methods of removing the business card from the cardbox. There is my *preferred method*, and then there is the *sure-fire method*.

Preferred Method: With your right hand's fingers, hold the cardbox by its narrow sides near the card-flap opening. Place your left hand on top of the business card, covering it completely. Allow the end of the business card closest to the stick figure's head to touch your left hand where your fingers meet the palm. With your left hand, pull the business card until it flips completely over toward you (FIG. 8). The business card should remain in the slit at all times. With your left hand, push the business card into the slit as far as it will go (FIG. 9). It should appear as if you've flipped the box over in your hands. Use the fingers of your right hand to open the box. Slowly remove the business card from within the cardbox, with your right hand, and show the prediction to your audience.

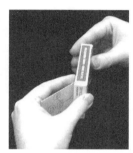

Figure 8

Figure 9

Sure-Fire Method: With the gimmicked side of the pack facing you, open the cardbox. Place your right hand's index finger inside the cardbox and your right hand's thumb outside the cardbox. Pinch your right hand's index finger and thumb together through the layers of the cardbox and business card stock (FIG. 10). Pretend to remove the business card from inside the cardbox and show the prediction to your audience. Watch your angles, of course. This should look convincing from your audience's perspective.

Figure 10

Both methods should convince your audience that the prediction was in the cardbox the entire time. The preferred method is visually more convincing but obviously more difficult to execute. The preferred method may appear cumbersome in writing, but it is silent and takes only a second to perform when executed correctly. The preferred method also allows a spectator to remove the business card from the box.

Once the prediction is removed from the cardbox, your audience will be stunned and amused by what it sees. Toss the cardbox aside or place it into your pocket, being careful not to call much attention to it. Give the business card as a souvenir to your sticky Post-It Note volunteer. For obvious reasons this effect makes a great closer; for one, mind-reading effects are hard to top, and two, the end of a routine is an excellent time to present someone with your calling card.

Bill Goldman also suggested adding personal touches to the stick figure drawing. For example, if the volunteer who is wearing the Post-It Notes is also wearing glasses, then draw glasses on the stick figure. Perhaps you could date the card afterward, so your volunteer would be able to tell friends exactly when this miracle took place. If it is the volunteer's birthday, then write "Happy Birthday" on the card. You get the idea. Make your business card something special that the volunteer would never want to lose.

Pieces of Eight

"Where your treasure is, there will be your heart also."
Matthew 6:21

<u>Effect</u>: Five half-dollars and a glass are introduced. The first two coins penetrate the bottom of the glass. The next two coins travel up one sleeve and down the other to the glass. The last coin vanishes and reappears under the glass. Then, as if that weren't enough, not one, not two, but three large coins magically appear from nowhere!

This is the only trick in the book for which you will have to spend a considerable amount of money if you want to perform the routine just as I do.

Required Items:

Figure 1

◆ 9-oz. double old-fashioned drinking glass made of crystal (FIG. 1). *I prefer a glass with a thick bottom, three inches in diameter.*

◆ A drawstring bag large enough to hold the glass inside. *I prefer to use an ornate bag with a pattern.*

◆ Five American half-dollars

◆ A three-inch jumbo half-dollar with a **shell coin** (FIG. 2). *The jumbo coin and shell I use have been nickel-plated for appearance purposes.*

◆ A squeeze coin purse (FIG. 3)

◆ A giant half-dollar coin with its holder (FIG. 4)

◆ Four large safety pins

Figure 2

Preparation: Prepare to produce the five half-dollars, or simply place them in the crystal glass. Place the glass into the drawstring bag and pull the mouth of the bag closed. *I prefer to roll up my shirt sleeves above my elbows before putting on my suit-jacket.* Put the giant coin into its special holder. Place the jumbo coin within its shell. Now place the shell coin(s) into the mouth of the squeeze coin purse.

Figure 3

Allow your right arm to relax naturally at your side. Reach under your jacket with your right hand and pinch the lining an inch above the bottom edge of your jacket. This is the exact spot where the bottom of the jumbo coin, within its shell, should be concealed. The face of the shell coin should rest against your jacket's lining. Pin the coin purse into the lining of your jacket accordingly.

Figure 4

Allow your left arm to relax naturally at your side. Reach under your jacket with your left hand and pinch the lining an inch above the bottom edge of your jacket. This is the exact spot where the bottom of the giant coin, within its holder, should be concealed. Pin the giant coin, in its holder, into the lining of your jacket accordingly.

Put on your jacket and make sure the large production coins are easily accessible when your arms relax naturally at your side. If not, then unfasten the pins and reposition the holders. Remember, if you button your jacket when setting up the trick, then button your jacket while performing it. The same rule applies if your jacket is unbuttoned.

Routine: Stand before your audience at the head of the table. Remove the glass from the bag. Lay the bag flat onto the table close by. Set the glass on top of the bag.

I. Introducing the Props:
Begin by producing the five half-dollars. This can be done magically or by simply dumping them out of the glass. Once the coins hit the table, I say, "Examine these coins all you like." As soon as someone reaches for them, I blurt out, "That's enough!" The audience laughs. Subconsciously, this use of humor will force the audience to analyze the coins with a sharp eye. Take back the coins and place them in front of the bag.

Typically, I'll hand one of the spectators the glass as I ask, "Is the glass solid? Say yes!" They grin as they reply, "Yes." I retort, "You're positive there are no mirrors, trapdoors or secret compartments?" Once again they respond, "Yes." These questions are formed to get a positive reply and to literally cut to the chase. After all, I do not want them handling the glass, then passing it around to others, risking the chance that it could be dropped and broken. Take back the glass and place it in front of the bag.

Pick up the bag with your right hand, allowing its mouth to pop open as you comment, "I know the bag looks mysterious, so reach in there . . . ." As soon as the lady I'm gesturing to reaches into the bag, I finish my sentence, ". . . and grab that spider!" Snort as you grab her fingers through the bag with the fingers of your left hand (FIG. 5). Once her reflexes take over, she will jerk her hand out of the bag and scream.

Figure 5

Bursts of laughter are sure to follow. Scaring your audience is not always bad. Normally, your so-called victim will be laughing the loudest. Scare tactics, when used correctly, capture your audience's undivided attention. Think about it; you're a magician: the audience should expect the unexpected.

All of the props for the routine have now been examined. *I know it seems we have taken the long road to accomplish a simple task, but just think of the fun you've had.* You have not performed any magic, yet the people in your audience are eagerly awaiting your next move while sitting on the edges of their seats. Psychologically, you have preconditioned your audience to react to everything that follows.

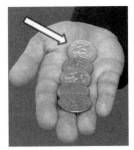

Figure 6

II. <u>Coin #1 Through the Bottom of the Glass—Visibly</u>:
Place the glass on top of the bag that is laid out flat on the table. Gather the five coins in your right hand. Bounce the coins around until one of them lands in the **Classic Palm** position (FIG. 6). Tilt your right hand down toward the tabletop and Classic Palm one of the half-dollars as the other coins fall to your right hand's fingertips (FIG. 7).

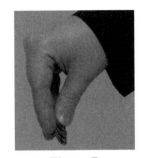

Figure 7

Casually toss the four halves held at your right hand's fingertips into your left hand. Close your left hand into a loose fist upon catching the coins. Turn your left fist up so that its thumb is on top. Use your left hand's thumb to push one of the coins about two-thirds of the way out of your fist (FIG. 8). Your right arm should relax and hang at your side.

Figure 8

Pick up the glass from the table with your right hand. The palm of your right hand should be directly over the mouth of the glass. Hold the glass over your left hand's fist and the exposed half-dollar. Smash the bottom of the glass on top of the left hand's exposed coin, forcing it back into your fist with the other three coins. Simultaneously release the coin in your right hand from the Classic Palm so that it will be heard to fall into the glass (FIG. 9).

Figure 9

The audience should believe that the coin has penetrated the bottom of the glass. The illusion is perfect. When timed correctly, this reality is created by the illusion of sight and sound. Verify the magic by dumping Coin #1 onto the bag for all to see. Applause is sure to follow.

III. Coin #2 Through the Bottom of the Glass:

Pick up Coin #1 and let it rest on the tips of your right hand's fingers. Your right hand should be palm up at this moment. Open your left hand to show the four half-dollars. Close your left hand around three of the coins, but allow one of them to hang out of the back of its fist (FIG. 10). You are preparing to execute the **Han Ping Chen** move over the mouth of the glass.

Figure 10

Your left hand should be positioned, fist down, directly over the glass that sits on the table. Turn your right hand palm down over the glass as you Classic Palm the coin that was just resting on its fingertips. Instantly release the coin from the back of your left hand's fist as you turn it to your left (FIG. 11). This move is called

Figure 11

the Han Ping Chen. It should look as if the coin in your right hand has been dumped into the glass. Actually, your closed left fist holds three coins, your right hand has a coin concealed in Classic Palm, and a coin is in the glass.

While doing the above, I jest, "You've just witnessed a solid penetrate a solid. Matter through matter. Actually, it's mind over matter. If you don't mind, it doesn't matter." I use humor here to help prepare for *Phase Three*. The things you say will help to cover the **sleights** you must perform. Your **patter** and body language contribute to the **misdirection** that will convince your audience they are witnessing real magic.

Now you will apparently cause the second coin to penetrate the bottom of the glass. Hold the glass up high with your right hand so that the coin in Classic Palm is positioned above the mouth of the glass once again. Remember that your left hand is holding three coins, supposedly four, in a loose fist. Open your left hand as you smash its coins against the bottom of the glass. Release the coin **palmed** in your right hand as soon as the coins in your left hand come in contact with the glass (FIG. 12).

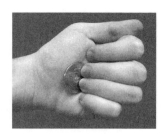

Figure 12

Your audience has just witnessed another coin penetrate the bottom of the glass. All should be awestruck. Dump the two coins out of the glass onto the bag and let the audience catch its breath. Keep your left hand open so all can see that it is holding three coins just as it should be.

IV. <u>Coin #3 From the Sleeve</u>:

Figure 13

Pick up the two coins on the table with your right hand. Place each of the coins in your right hand into the Classic Palm. Bounce the three coins around in your left hand and close it around one of the coins while holding the other two outside the fist as you turn the fist downward. Execute the Han Ping Chen move as you pretend to throw the coins in your right hand into the glass (FIG. 13). Actually, the two coins hanging out of the back of your left hand's fist should fall into the glass.

As I do the above Han Ping Chen sequence, I suggest to someone, "I know what you are thinking. You are wondering how Diamond Jim does this." Then I look toward a skeptic in the crowd as I say, "And you're thinking, 'Why does Diamond Jim do this?'" The audience laughs as the switch of the two coins is made.

Figure 14

Pretend to be loading a coin from your left hand into your left sleeve as you grip the cuff of the sleeve. Say, "Coin #3 goes up this sleeve, across my shoulders, and down this sleeve." Pick up the glass with your right hand and release just one of the coins from Classic Palm (FIG. 14). In the audience's eyes, Coin #3 has magically traveled to the glass. All should be amused.

V. <u>Coin #4 From the Sleeve—Visibly</u>:

Place the glass nearby on the table. Leave the three half-dollars in the glass momentarily. One half-dollar is hidden in your right hand. Your audience should believe that you have two coins in your left hand, but there is only one. You are almost ready to make Coin #4 travel to the glass.

Figure 15

Raise your lower right arm as you use your right hand to point toward your upper left arm. Say, "Coin #4, like #3, travels up my sleeve . . ." (FIG. 15). As you say these words, let the coin fall from your right hand into its sleeve. If you want to, you can open your left hand to show the single coin that remains, as added misdirection. Keep the right arm raised as you finish your sentence, " . . . across my shoulders once again and down to the glass."

Tilt the mouth of your right sleeve toward the mouth of the glass. Make it clear that your right hand is empty as you hold it open with your palm out. Allow the coin to fall a considerable distance into the glass from your right sleeve (FIG. 16). The jaws of your spectators should drop at this point. Tilt the glass to rest on its side and allow two or three of the four coins to fall out of the glass onto the bag.

Figure 16

VI. Coin #5 Interlude:

Offer an amusing explanation: "Do you know how I do this stuff? I train my coins." Show Coin #5 in your right hand as you say, "This coin, when it was just a baby, just a nickel, I taught it how to walk." **Walk the coin** across the knuckles of your left hand (FIG. 17). Walk the coin backward across your knuckles as you joke, "Then as it got older, I taught it how to moon-walk" (FIG. 18). The spectators always smile here.

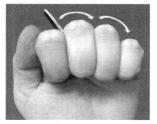

Figure 17

Continue pulling their legs by saying, "Then when it matured, it earned its wings." Display the eagle on the back of the coin while holding it in your right hand. Separate your two hands a couple of feet by holding your right hand near your waist, with your left hand directly above it. Execute the **Muscle Pass** with your right hand, causing the half-dollar to fly upward into your left hand (FIG. 19). During this action I say, "See, I've taught it how to fly." I'll usually put the coin back into my right hand and do the Muscle Pass again as I say, "This coin was trained to fall up." *I recommend doing the Muscle Pass sequence a second time, as I've suggested, for those in your audience who might have blinked the first time.*

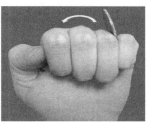

Figure 18

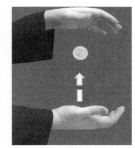

Figure 19

VII. Coin #5 Vanishes and Reappears:

Execute the **Retention of Vision Vanish** while pretending to put the coin in your left hand (FIG. 20). The coin should ultimately be hidden in the Classic Palm position in your right hand. Say, "Keep your eye on

Figure 20

this coin. I've got an idea. Hold my wrist so it doesn't get away or go up my sleeve." Gesture with your left hand's fist by holding it out. Sometimes, as a subtlety, I'll grab my left wrist with my guilty right hand, to suggest that it's apparently empty.

Figure 21

Move your right hand toward the glass to pick it up. As your right hand touches the bottom of the glass, allow the coin palmed in your hand to fall into **Finger Rest** position. The coin will be hidden from your audience by the thick bottom of the glass (FIG. 21). Tilt the glass up onto your right hand's fingertips, covering the coin. If the coin in your right hand makes a clicking noise against the glass, it shouldn't matter. After all, there is a coin or two in the glass that could have made a similar noise.

Ask someone nearby to pick up the coins on the bag and toss them into the glass. Ask the same person to make sure there are only four coins in the glass. After the spectator concurs, place the hidden coin in your right hand onto the bag, with the glass on top of it. Direct all attention to your left hand.

Wiggle the fingers of your left hand as if you are fidgeting with the coin inside it. Open your left hand's fingers as you ask, "Did you see it go? It's not in my hands." Show your hands. Continue, "It's not up my sleeves," as you roll up your jacket's sleeves. Finish by saying, "It's not even in the glass. Do you want to know where it is? Look under the glass."

VIII. <u>Big Coin is Produced</u>:

Allow your right arm to relax naturally at your side. As someone lifts the glass, steal the jumbo coin in its shell from under your jacket. Hold the jumbo coin(s) with the ring finger and thumb of your right hand (FIG. 22). The little finger of your right hand will keep the large coin from falling out of its shell. All attention will be focused on the coin under the glass.

Figure 22

With your left hand, take the glass from the spectator. Place the glass on top of the jumbo coin(s) in your right hand as you direct the audience's attention to the coin on the table. Pick up the coin on the table with your left hand as your right hand places its contents on top of the bag. For a little added misdirection you might ask everyone, "Have you ever seen a trick coin before?" All should fix their gaze on the coin in your left hand.

Figure 23

As I hold the half-dollar in my left hand high for all to see, I say, "This is not one. As a rule, I don't use trick coins. Have you ever seen them? They're too big. You can't hide them in your hand." After having said that, reach for the bottom of the glass with your right hand. Toss Coin #5 into the glass with the others. Carefully lift the shell off the jumbo coin while taking the glass away (FIG. 23). Your audience will be stunned by the production of this large coin. Pick up the large metal coin with your left hand and bang it on the table to reinforce the magic.

IX. Second Big Coin is Produced:
Place the glass and shell that are in your right hand back onto the bag. Accept your applause for the production of the first large coin. Say, "Did you like that? It's my favorite part." Place the jumbo half-dollar aside or into a pocket. Inquire, "Would you like me to do it again?" Your audience will insist, "YES!" Snap your fingers, show that your hands are empty, and lift the glass into the air with either hand.

Put down the glass beside the bag and pick up the second large coin. Bang the shell coin on the table, being careful not to reveal the fact that it's hollow. Place the second jumbo coin aside or into a pocket. Your audience will be falling out of their chairs about now. Remember, your sleeves are pushed up, so no one should be able to create an explanation for what just happened.

X. FINALE—Giant Coin is Produced:
You are about to produce the last coin. The audience thought that the routine was over when Coin #5 appeared under the glass. The production of the first large coin probably threw them. The second large coin left them speechless. Now the giant coin is going to kill them.

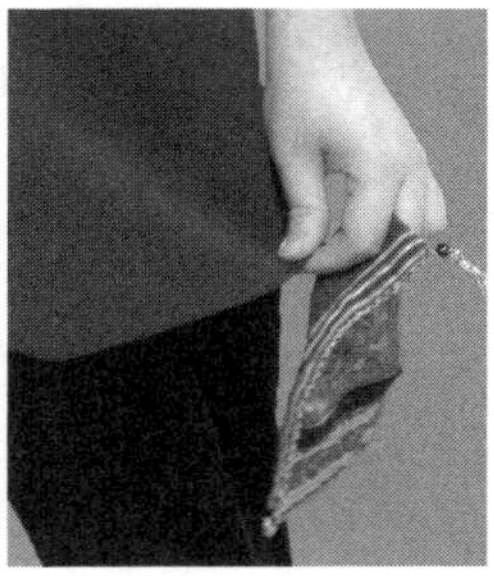

As you are receiving your applause and taking a bow, pick up the bag with your left hand. The bottom of the bag should be held by the crotch of your left hand's index finger and thumb. Allow your left arm to relax naturally at your side. Steal the giant coin from under your jacket with your left hand (FIG. 24). The coin should remain hidden

Figure 24

behind the bag. To help misdirect this action, simply raise the glass in your right hand as if you are toasting your audience.

Place the glass on the table as you say, "Oh! Wait a minute. . . . I forgot to mention that this routine is called Pieces of Eight." Hold the corners of the bag with each hand while hiding the giant coin behind it (FIG. 25). The mouth of the bag should be directed toward the table. Look up as if you are calculating numbers in your head as you say, "Let's see. There were five coins to begin with, plus the two big ones at the end. Hmm . . . that makes seven."

Figure 25

Shake the bag over the table and drop the coin out from behind the bag as you say, "And there's eight!" From the audience's perspective, it should look as if the giant coin falls from the bag. Everyone in the place should be completely bamboozled at this point. Place the glass and regular coins back into the bag as a subtle reminder that the bag was otherwise empty at the beginning of the routine.

This is a very strong routine that should be used as a closer. This routine has many applause cues built in, so try not to step on them. If I had to choose one effect to perform for a group, it would be my routine Pieces of Eight. So much happens during this effect that it qualifies you not only as a skilled magician but also as a true entertainer.

<u>Why use the particular glass mentioned?</u> The glass should be made of crystal so that it is less likely to crack during the routine. Drinking glasses made of glass break quite often during this routine if you toss coins into them. The width of the bottom of the glass should be the same size as your jumbo coin and shell. The width is important because it should completely conceal your loads until you are ready to reveal them. A fancy glass, like the one used here, can be purchased at any good store that sells dining ware, such as Crate & Barrel.

<u>Why produce the large coins</u>? The routine might survive without the production of the large coins. In my opinion, the routine is done just as an excuse to produce the large coins. Try the routine both producing and without producing the large coins, and you will see the difference in your

audience's reaction. The large coins can be purchased from my website www.diamond-jim.com.

<u>Why use the bag</u>? This routine evolved tableside in restaurants. Usually I'll end a close-up performance with the routine Pieces of Eight. The bag obviously conceals the glass and its contents until you are ready to perform the effect. An empty glass sitting on a dining table has a good chance of being taken away by the busboy or wait staff. Placing the bag around the glass prevents patrons from treating it like a tip jar by tossing their pocket change into it.

The bag also adds an element of mystery and a touch of class to the effect. After being removed from around the glass, the bag makes an excellent close-up mat upon which to perform. As a mat, the bag will prohibit coins from clicking on the table and will make things easier to pick up. Using the bag as a mat also defines your territory on the table and the area where the magic will happen.

Since the bag originally held the glass, everyone will be amazed when you produce the giant coin from within it. The bag may be used to polish the glass and to wipe away fingerprints or other stains. The bag serves many purposes. Those who know me well can probably guess what I think is the most important reason for using the bag. Think back to the beginning of the routine. Remember the spider gag? That's the reason!

The Birthday Bill

"All men dream: but not equally. Those who dream by night in the dusty recesses of their minds wake in the day to find that it was vanity: but the dreamers of the day are dangerous men, for they may act their dreams with open eyes, to make it possible."
T.E. Lawrence
Seven Pillars of Wisdom

Effect: The magician offers to teach the birthday person a magic trick with a borrowed $1 bill. The magician teaches the spectator the old bit where the portrait of George Washington magically turns over on the face of the bill. The magician proclaims, "I will change the borrowed bill into a $100 bill with the wave of my magic wand!" The magician searches his pockets for a wand, but produces a hole-puncher instead. The magician waves the hole-puncher around the folded $1 bill and seems dismayed. Confused, he opens the bill, revealing the punched-out message "Happy B-day." The bill is given to the birthday person as a souvenir.

Required Items:
- ◆ A pencil
- ◆ A dollar bill
- ◆ A safety pin
- ◆ A hole-puncher
- ◆ Some paper clips
- ◆ A pair of scissors
- ◆ A brightly colored piece of posterboard

Figure 1

Preparation: First, practice punching out words that are readable into a piece of paper with the hole-puncher (FIG. 1). After practicing, cut out a piece of posterboard the exact size of a dollar bill. Punch out the message "HAPPY B-DAY" into the posterboard (FIG. 2). The position of the abbreviation "B-DAY" is crucial to the handling of the effect.

Figure 2

Place a $1 bill, face up, behind the posterboard stencil you have created. Carefully punch out the words "HAPPY B-DAY." Try not to punch out more of your stencil when preparing the dollar bill. Save the circular punch-outs from the bill and keep them nearby. Prepare several of these punched-out bills at one time.

Figure 3

You will need to fold the bill into eighths (FIG. 3). It is important that only the back of the bill is showing when the folds are complete. Hold the bill face out and face up so the punched-out message is easy to read from the audience's perspective. Fold the bill in half lengthwise, then in half widthwise, then in half lengthwise once again. One side of the folded packet should resemble FIG. 3. If one side of your folded bill does not look like FIG. 3, then refold it until it does. Be sure that your folded creases are firm so the bill will remain in its tidy square packet.

Hold the folded bill so the upside-down printed "ONE" is away from you. Look at the bill from above and notice the number of pockets created by the folds. Open one of the first few pockets farthest from you and place half of the bill's punch-outs inside. Fasten a paper clip three-fourths of the way onto the bill, securing the punch-outs inside (FIG. 4).

Figure 4

Stand up and allow your left arm to relax naturally at your side. Curl your left fingers up and under your jacket. The area where your left fingers are touching is the same area that you want the folded bill to be located (FIG. 5). If your jacket is unbuttoned when you set up the trick, you must unbutton it when you perform the effect. The same applies if the jacket is buttoned; button it when you perform.

Figure 5

Run the safety pin through the paper clip and fasten the folded bill in the aforementioned area. Be sure the upside-down printed "ONE" is facing toward the audience. The dollar should be hanging about an inch from the bottom edge of your jacket (FIG. 6). Place the hole-puncher into your outside right jacket pocket, and you are ready to begin.

Figure 6

Routine: Once you have discovered a birthday person in the crowd, explain that you intend to break the magician's code on this special occasion and teach him or her a magic trick. Ask to borrow a $1 bill from someone other than the birthday person. Teach the group how to do the old trick, in which the portrait of **George Washington Flips Over** on the face of the bill. After you have explained how to do the trick, hand the birthday person the dollar bill to repeat what he or she has just learned. As the birthday person attempts to perform the trick, this provides plenty of **misdirection**. Secretly, with your left hand, remove the prepared bill from under your jacket and place it into **Finger Palm** (FIG. 7).

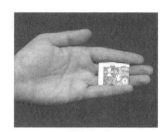

Figure 7

Take back the dollar bill and say, "Let me show you once more how to perform this so you will never forget how it's done." As you fold the bill, be careful not to expose the punched-out bill that is Finger Palmed in your left hand. This time, begin folding the borrowed bill into eighths, so that it resembles the punched-out bill, as shown in FIG. 3. As you make the last fold, secretly Finger Palm the

Figure 8

borrowed bill in your right hand as you push the punched-out bill into view (FIG. 8). This last step is not as difficult as it seems in writing. The audience is not expecting a switch. The audience believes that you are teaching someone how to do a trick, so your spectators' defenses are down.

Say, "Better yet, what if I could change this $1 bill into a $100 bill for you to keep?" The audience as well as the birthday person usually accepts this kind offer with a big smile. Reply, "If I have my magic wand on me, then I will be glad to do it." Hold the punched-out bill by one of its corners with the index finger and thumb of your left hand so that it remains in plain view. With your right hand go into a pocket to ditch the folded borrowed bill. Act as if you are searching for a magic wand. Dismayed, bring out the hole-puncher and say, "Oh, well, maybe *this* will work?!?" Wave the hole-puncher around the punched-out bill in a mystical manner. Place the hole-puncher back into your pocket as you stare at the bill. The audience can plainly see the printed upside-down "ONE" on the bill.

Look at the audience as you say, "Well, this didn't work exactly as I planned it, but anyhow, HAPPY BIRTHDAY!" Unfold the bill so the message is upright and easy for the audience to read. As the bill is unfolded, the punch-outs cascade onto the table, creating an unforgettable moment. Although the spectators were expecting the transformation of a $1 bill into a $100 bill, they should be just as surprised. *I promise you this; the birthday person will keep this as a souvenir much longer than he or she would have kept the $100.*

The Birthday Bill has many appealing qualities within the act of a close-up magician. First, it seems that you are performing this effect completely **impromptu***. The effect resets quickly, assuming that you have prepared several bills at one time, as I instructed earlier. The effect is frozen in time, so that each time the birthday person looks at the bill, it will bring back memories of that special day as well as the magician who performed the miracle. Finally, you are out just the expense of the posterboard and the time it took to prepare the effect, since you get to keep the actual borrowed bill.*

When you are performing the effect, make it your own. Adopt a style and handling that best suits you. Be creative. Obviously, other messages could be revealed on the dollar, such as "HAPPY ANNIV", "MERRY XMAS", "SIX OF CLUBS, ",etc.

I would also like to give credit to Timothy Wenk for creating Punchline, an effect in which a punched-out message appears in a large folded piece of paper. I believe Mr. Wenk would agree that his effect was not designed for close-up use. His handling is completely different, and the use of a dollar bill was never mentioned in his original routine. Although I have never performed Mr. Wenk's Punchline effect, I would like to thank him for planting the seed. His genius helped foster what I consider to be the most commercial trick in my book.

Glossary

Apparatus: The equipment a magician uses to perform his **effects** or **tricks**.

Assistant: Someone who helps the magician with part of his act. This person could be the magician's partner or merely a spectator from the audience.

Back (of the Card): The side of a playing card opposite the **face** (FIG. 1).

Figure 1

Bar Bet: Placing a small wager on a task that may or may not be possible to complete. *For examples, see the **routines** Three Burnt Matches, Nimble Corks and Wise Guys Can't Count.*

Block (of Cards): A **squared packet** of cards. The actual number of cards in a block depends on the **routine**.

Bobo Switch: A **sleight-of-hand** switch where an object is tossed into the hand and exchanged for another object.

Method: For the sake of clarity, assume you are using a silver half-dollar and a copper English penny. The English penny is concealed in the **Finger Palm** position in your right hand. The half-dollar is displayed in your open left hand (FIG. 2).

Figure 2

Pick up the half-dollar with the first two fingers and thumb of your right hand (FIG. 3). Toss the half-dollar into your left hand and close the fingers around it. This *retrieving and tossing* action is generally repeated once again to establish a pattern. Now, for the third time, retrieve the half-dollar, as shown in FIG. 3, and prepare for the switch.

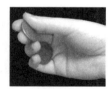

Figure 3

When you are ready to make the switch, merely open the second, third and fourth fingers of your right hand slightly, releasing the copper coin. The half-dollar should be retained with the index finger and thumb of your right hand (FIG. 4). Catch the copper coin in your left hand, closing its fingers

Figure 4

143

around it. At this point, the half-dollar should be concealed from the audience's view by the outstretched fingers of your right hand.

Only a slight movement is necessary to place the half-dollar in the Finger Palm position, where it is typically retained. The right arm is usually allowed to rest at one's side after the switch. Open your left hand at will to show that the magical transformation has taken place. The switch should be mastered so that all moves appear to blend into one action. The audience should be convinced that you have tossed the same coin into your left hand—until the moment you reveal the transformation. Your right hand will be suspected of hiding the half-dollar, so be prepared to prove otherwise.

Bobo's book, Modern Coin Magic, *is considered to be the "Bible of Coin Sleights" by most students of magic. Although Bobo was a world-renowned magician and author of magical literature, he is best known for his switch. When learning this universal maneuver that bears his name, remember Bobo's own words: "Learn this sleight and you will have a valuable tool that will serve you well as long as you do close-up magic."*

Bottom (of the Deck): The lowermost card or portion of the deck, sometimes referred to as the **face** of the deck (FIG. 5).

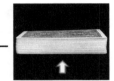

Figure 5

Break: A slight opening secretly held in the back of a deck of cards (FIG. 6).

Figure 6

Break Force: A means of **forcing** a card on a spectator. Start by holding a **break** in the back of the deck above the card you wish to force (FIG. 6). **Riffle** the front left corner of the deck with your left thumb as you instruct someone, "Please call stop at any time" (FIG. 7). Once the spectator calls stop, use your right hand to lift all of the cards above the break. As you separate the halves of the deck, it is best to tilt your hands forward at this moment so your audience doesn't see exactly where the cards are **cut**. When this is done properly and timed right, it should appear that you have separated the pack where your audience has requested. The **force card** is then shown to the audience.

Figure 7

Other great forces can be found in 202 Methods of Forcing *by Theodore Annemann.*

Breather Card: A **gaffed** creased card used as a locator or **key card** in a deck. *The breather card shown here is also known as a "Will De Seive Gimmick."*

Making a breather card is simple. First you must decide whether the creases should be in the front or back of the playing card. Regardless, it's wise to use a **face card** or a card with a printed pattern to camouflage the creased impressions. *For the reason given, I prefer to use Jokers as breathers.*

The best tool to make impressions in your breather card is an American quarter. When making a *convex* breather, put three impressions of a quarter into the **back** of the card (FIG. 8). When making a *concave* breather, put three impressions into the **face** of the card. These impressions will last a long time if you press them in firmly.

Figure 8

Bridge: A **flourish** used to **square** a deck of cards that has just been **shuffled**. The cards are bowed into the shape of a bridge and forced together as shown in FIG. 9.

Figure 9

Change: An **effect** in which one item is magically transformed into another.

Change Bag: A **gimmicked** cloth bag used by magicians to switch out or **produce** or **vanish** items. *Check your local magic store to find out more about this multipurpose **apparatus**.*

Charlier (Pass or Cut): This is a very impressive **one-handed cut**. Start by holding the deck along its long edges, **face down** over your palm with either hand (FIG. 10). Arch your thumb slightly upward to allow the bottom half of the deck to fall onto your palm (FIG. 11). Push the bottom half of the deck up and over the edge of the top half with your index finger. Your other fingers should remain straight and continue to hold the top half of the deck in place (FIG. 12).

Figure 10

Figure 11

As the bottom half comes up and over the top half, let go with your thumb so that the top half drops onto your palm under the bottom half. Move your index finger out from under the

Figure 12

deck. Finish by **squaring** the edges of the pack. *Since I am right-handed, I hold the deck in my left hand. This allows my right hand to deal cards or perform other functions. However, you should use whichever hand makes sense for you. For more information on this one-hand cutting technique, see the following:*

Now You See It, Now You Don't *by Bill Tarr*
Mark Wilson's Complete Course in Magic *by Mark Wilson and Walter Gibson*

Cigarette Paper Tear: An old classic of **close-up** magic in which a small piece of cigarette paper is torn into several pieces and then restored to its original condition while in the magician's hands.

Classic Palm: A **sleight** that allows the magician to conceal a coin or coins in his hand.

This is one of the oldest coin concealments in the history of **sleight-of-hand** magic. In my opinion, it also happens to be the most valuable sleight that a **close-up** magician can learn. Once a magician has learned and perfected this concealment, he will find that, by comparison, other sleights are simple to master.

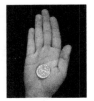

Figure 13

Method: Place the coin(s) into the center of your palm and hold them there using only the muscles in your hand (FIG. 13). *I prefer using American half-dollars.* The muscles used to hold the coin(s) in place are located at the base of your thumb and little finger. This sleight may seem difficult to do at first, but it will become easier with practice.

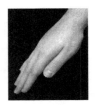

Figure 14

Strive to palm the coin(s) in a relaxed hand (FIG. 14) rather than in a hand that looks cramped or contorted (FIG. 15). J. B. Bobo taught, *"A coin is not a heavy object, so hold it lightly and the hand will appear natural. Actually it should be held so loosely that a mere tap with the other hand will dislodge it."*

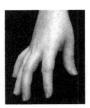

Figure 15

Placing the coin(s) into Classic Palm: *I have listed a few ways to place the coin(s) into Classic Palm.* The method that you choose should depend on the **effect** that you are performing:

- ◆ <u>Two Hands</u>: Use your other hand to place the coin(s) into the Classic Palm position (FIG. 16).
- ◆ <u>One Hand</u>: Bounce the coin(s) in your hand until they land in Classic Palm position.
- ◆ <u>One Hand</u>: Allow the coin(s) to rest on the tips of the ring and middle fingers of your hand. The coin(s) can then be pressed into Classic Palm, as your hand turns down (FIG. 17).

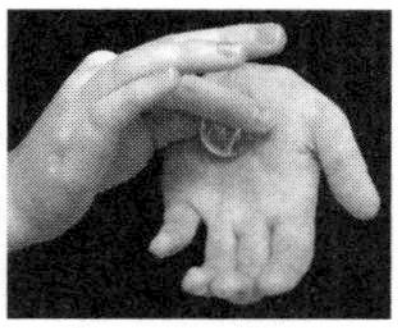

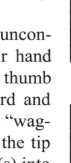

Figure 16

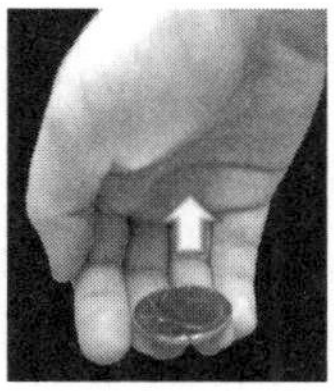

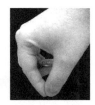

Figure 17

When performing the last method, many magicians will unconsciously allow their thumbs to outstretch, making their hand appear guilty of foul play (FIG. 18). The action of your thumb extending out while palming the coin(s) looks awkward and calls attention to your guilty hand. This is known as the "wagging thumb syndrome". To overcome it, simply touch the tip of your thumb to your index finger as you press the coin(s) into your palm with the ring and middle fingers of your guilty hand (FIG. 19).

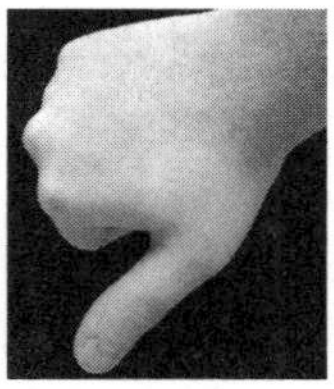

Figure 18

If you wish the audience to believe that your guilty hand is empty, then you must act as if it is empty. Use your guilty hand to pick up a magic wand, move a glass, grab a spectator's arm, etc. To prevent the palmed coin(s) from being seen, simply keep the palm of your hand directed toward your body.

Figure 19

Remember to be natural when practicing and performing this sleight. J. B. Bobo said it best: *"Only when the hand looks natural will it be above suspicion. The ability to palm a coin should be mastered first; naturalness will come later."* I could quote all of what J. B. Bobo had to say about the Classic Palm, but I encourage you to buy and read his book, Modern Coin Magic. Appropriately, you will find the instructions for the Classic Palm on page one of Bobo's book.

Click Pass: This **sleight** is used to convince an audience that the magician has more coins in his hand than he really does. We will use two coins in this example. Execute a coin vanish (such as the **Retention of Vision Vanish**) and **Classic Palm** the hidden coin in your right hand. Pick up the second coin with your right hand and hold it momentarily in the **Finger Rest** position.

Your left hand should open just slightly to receive the coin from your right hand. Your right hand should release the Classic Palmed coin. As the coin falls, it should strike the coin resting on the tips of your right hand's fingers and then fall into your awaiting left hand (FIG. 20). Your left hand should immediately close into a fist and pull away as your right arm relaxes at your side.

Figure 20

Your audience should believe that both coins are in your left hand. Actually, you have a coin in each hand. Going through the motions of placing a coin into your hand can be convincing. This **sleight** is unique, since it gives the illusion of sight and sound. To succeed at this coin sleight, as well as others, you must perform it quickly but effortlessly. *For further instructions, see* Modern Coin Magic *by J. B. Bobo.*

Closer: An **effect** or **routine** used to end a magic act.

Close-Up: The type of magic performed up close and personal. Close-up magicians perform for small audiences using things they carry in their pockets or in a small case. Professionals may perform this type of magic in restaurants from table to table. *See also strolling, table-hopping, and walk-around.*

Coins Across: A **routine** in which four coins are each placed in their own corner and caused magically to join one another at one corner. *This routine is sometimes called a matrix.*

Coins Through Table: A **routine** in which coins seem to magically penetrate the surface of a table. *For a routine example, see Trapdoor Coins.*

Con: The word is short for "confidence game." A swindle in which someone cheats at gambling or persuades others to participate in an activity in which they have a good chance of losing something of value.

Con Man: A person who use **cons**. *See also wise guy.*

Control: To maintain a selected card or cards secretly to various parts of the deck, usually to the **top** or **bottom**. This term also refers to the magician's ability to keep track of, or maintain control of, a card during a **shuffling** or **cutting** sequence. *For examples, see the Overhand or Hindu Shuffle.*

Cut: The action of removing a **packet** or **block** from the **top** of the deck and placing it beside the lower portion. *Completing the cut* consists of placing the lower portion on top of the upper portion.

Cut Deeper Force: A method for causing someone to select the card you desire. Secretly place your **force card** on **top** of the deck. Let's assume your force card is the 7♦. Once you're prepared to **force** the card, have someone **cut** off a third or half of the cards from the tabled deck. Ask the spectator to turn the cut-off **packet face up** on top of the balance of the deck.

Have someone cut even deeper into the deck, past the face-up cards, and remove them from the tabled deck. Ask the volunteer to turn the packet of cards face over and to place them back onto the balance of the deck. Explain that the first **face-down** card he or she should come to will be the selected card. **Fan** or spread the cards so the volunteer can remove the first face-down card. This card will be your force card, the 7♦.

Other great forces can be found in 202 Methods of Forcing *by Theodore Annemann.*

Dancing Handkerchief: A classic of **stage** magic in which a handkerchief is made to dance, contort and float while being accompanied by music and the direction of a magician.

Dealer's Grip: The grip one uses to hold a pack of cards in a natural dealing position. When using your left hand, grasp the pack as shown in FIG. 21.

Figure 21

Double: Two cards held together and shown as one.

Double-lift: The action of showing two cards as one. To execute a double-lift, hold the deck in a natural position, such as the **Dealer's Grip**, in your left hand (FIG. 21). Using your right hand's thumb, **riffle** up the back of the pack until you get to the top two cards (FIG. 22). Lifting the two cards as one is known as a **double**. Obviously, this takes some practice to perform discreetly. There are different ways of performing the same **sleight**, but if you are reading this, then it is a good place to start. *To further your knowledge of this common card sleight as well as others, read the book* The Royal Road to Card Magic *by Jean Hugard and Frederick Braue.*

Figure 22

Dovetail Shuffle: The most common method for mixing a pack of cards. Typically, half of the deck is held lengthwise in each hand. The cards should be **riffling** off the tips of both thumbs, one at a time or in small clumps, while interlacing with one another (FIG. 23). After the cards are mixed in this fashion, you usually push the pack together and **square** the cards. Sometimes, you might complete this shuffle by executing the **Bridge**.

Figure 23

Down's Change: A **sleight-of-hand** technique used to **change** one card to another. Typically, the deck is held **face up** in the **Dealer's Grip** before executing the Down's Change. Before starting, you should have a **break** under the **double** you are holding on the **face** of the deck. Normally, only your little finger should be used when getting a break in the deck. In this case, your index, middle and ring fingers should be curled around the deck and in between the face of the deck and your double (FIG. 24). The double should rest on top of the fingernails of your index, middle and ring fingers.

Figure 24

For this example we will say the back card of your double is the Ace of Spades and the front card of your double is a Joker. Pull your double halfway off the face of the deck with your right hand. Pivot your double diagonally to your right and hold it in that position momentarily with your left thumb (FIG. 25). The card is angled away from the balance of the deck to make the Down's Change easier to perform. Now you are ready to switch the card your audience sees (Joker) with the card underneath it (Ace of Spades).

Figure 25

Hold the cards in your left hand in the same position as you execute the following movements. Turn your left hand from palm up to palm down as you stretch its fingers out straight. Straightening your left hand's fingers should pull the back

Figure 26

of your double (Ace of Spades) away from the deck to be placed on the table (FIG. 26). Your audience should see only the back of this card (Ace of Spades). While doing this, your left hand's thumb should pull the face of your double (Joker) toward the face of the deck.

When you are performing the Down's Change, it should look as if you are simply using one hand to remove a card from the face of the deck in order to place it **face down** on the table. Just after the change has been done, you should hide the card on the face of the deck by placing the entire pack face down somewhere. Sometime afterward, reveal that the face-down card on the table has transformed into another card. This change will take some practice to execute discreetly. When practicing, try to make sure that the cards do not make any tell-tale noises to give away what you are actually doing.

Dribbling Cards: This is a **flourish** used with cards to make them cascade from one hand into the other. Squeeze the cards off the **bottom** of the deck and catch them with your other hand (FIG. 27). When this is done perfectly, the cards will shoot one at a time from the bottom of the deck. To enhance this flourish, pull your hands as far apart as you can while dribbling and catching the cards.

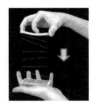

Figure 27

Effect: A **routine** performed by a magician described, as if it were seen through the audience's eyes.

Face (of Card or Deck): The face of a card reveals its suit and value (FIG. 28).

Figure 28

Face Card(s): The Jacks, Queens and Kings in a deck of cards. Also referred to as *picture or court cards*.

Face Down: The number or picture side of a card is facing downward so that the card's identity is unknown (FIG. 29). Those looking at the card will see only the **back** of the card.

Figure 29

Face Up: The number or picture side of a card is facing upward so that the card's identity is known (FIG. 28).

False Cut: The action of pretending to **cut** a pack of cards in which to mix them when the cards actually remain in the same order. *See the **Swing False Cut**.*

False Shuffle: The action of pretending to **shuffle** a pack of cards when actually the cards remain in the same order. *See the **Riffle False Shuffle**.*

Fan: Cards spread in the magician's hands to resemble an oriental fan (FIG. 30). This **sleight** is useful when asking

Figure 30

someone to select a card. *As a **flourish**, card fans usually separate amateur magicians from the professionals.*

Fanning Cards: The method that I am about to teach is better known as a Thumb Fan. *Having taught myself this **flourish**, I have learned to execute a fan with my index finger rather than my thumb.* Another popular fanning technique is called the Pressure Fan. *I utilize part of the Pressure Fan technique by **springing the cards** before I execute my fan.* You will find that the better the quality of your cards, the more evenly your card fans will spread.

Figure 31

Begin by holding the deck in your left hand. The deck should be pivoted at an angle and held as shown in FIG. 31. The bottom right corner of the deck is held by your left hand's thumb, which will apply pressure to this corner as you begin fanning the cards. Wrap your right hand's index finger over the top left corner of the deck. Use this finger to spread the cards to your right in a circular motion (FIG. 32). Apply pressure with your left hand's thumb and your right hand's index finger in order to help the cards spread evenly.

Figure 32

From the front, your card fan should look like the illustration in FIG. 30. Needless to say, fanning cards takes much practice. The more you practice fanning, the better you will get. Experiment by making adjustments in your grip to develop a handling technique that works for you. Try to make the card fan as large as possible. For more references on fanning, see the following:

Now You See It, Now You Don't by Bill Tarr
Mark Wilson's Complete Course in Magic by Mark Wilson and Walter Gibson

Finger Flinging: Difficult card **sleights** or **flourishes** performed by card-handlers and magicians. In a finger-flinging **effect**, cards are typically seen spinning or flying or zipping from here to there. *See my Diamond's Dazzler **routine** for an example.*

Finger Grip: The coin-sized object is held by the ends of the index and pinkie fingers. The object should rest flat against your ring and middle fingers (FIG. 33). This **sleight** is referred to as the Front Finger Hold in Bobo's *Modern Coin Magic*. *Half-dollars work best for me when using this sleight.*

Figure 33

Finger Palm: This is the most natural coin concealment there is. The coin or small object should be held by the base of your curled ring and middle fingers, as shown in FIG. 34. For more tips on this **sleight**, see Bobo's *Modern Coin Magic*.

Figure 34

Finger Rest: This hold is used to hide a small object in your hand and depends on your being aware of any bad angles. Most often your arm is relaxed at your side when performing this **sleight**. The object to be hidden should rest on the tips of your slightly curled ring and middle fingers (FIG. 35).

Figure 35

Flash Paper: A highly flammable tissue paper treated with nitric acid. This special paper is sold in most magic or theatrical supply shops.

Flourish: Any display of skill while performing magic. *Some examples of flourishes would be **fanning cards**, **springing cards** and **walking a coin**.*

Force or **Forcing**: A technique in which the selection of an object, usually a card, is forced on a spectator who is under the impression that he is making a free choice. *See the **Break, Cut Deeper, Hindu Shuffle,** and **Reversed Card** forces for examples.*

Force Card: A certain card that is selected, or soon to be selected, seemingly by a spectator, but actually by the magician's choice. Cards are forced in **routines** in which the outcome of an **effect** is dependent upon a certain card being chosen.

Four Ace Routine: A **routine** that focuses on or uses only the four Aces.

French Drop: A **sleight** used to make a small object vanish. Start by holding the object by the tips of the thumb and middle fingers of your left hand. Your right hand should move in closer to take the object (FIG. 36). Apparently, your right hand takes the object. Actually, under cover of your right hand, the object falls into the cupped fingers of your left hand.

Figure 36

Your left arm relaxes at your side while your right arm moves toward the audience with a closed fist. Typically, your right hand is shown empty, and the audience assumes that the object has vanished. *Obviously, this sleight cannot stand alone, or the audience will suspect your other hand. When this* *maneuver is used in conjunction with other sleights during a **routine**, it can be very convincing. For further instructions on this old technique, see the following:*

Now You See It, Now You Don't *by Bill Tarr*
Mark Wilson's Complete Course in Magic *by Mark Wilson and Walter Gibson*

Gaff or **Gaffed**: A term used by magicians to refer to a **gimmick** or a specially prepared piece of **apparatus**. Gaffed items are known to the magician, yet unseen by the audience.

Gag: A harmless practical joke.

George Washington Flips Over Trick: An **impromptu effect** in which the portrait of the President flips upside down on a $1 bill. This is a great giveaway **trick** to teach someone. Begin by holding the face of the bill right side up for your audience to see. You should be looking at the back of the bill while performing the trick.

Fold the left side of the bill to your right so that the portrait of George Washington is hidden inside the fold. Once the edges of the bill are lined up, crease the fold that runs down the center of the bill (FIG. 37). Fold the top half of the bill toward your audience lengthwise. The bill should then be folded into fourths (FIG. 38). Crease the folds after aligning the edges once again. Fold the left half of the bill to your right so that the bill is in eighths. Crease all the folds one last time to create a tidy square packet (FIG. 39). At this moment the magician usually snaps his fingers or says a magic word, supposedly putting a spell on the money.

Figure 37

Figure 38

Figure 39

Next, begin the magic unfolding sequence. The last fold that you made, which folded the bill into eighths, should be undone. The bill will appear to be in fourths again (FIG. 38). As you unfold the bill from being folded into fourths, use your thumbs to lift the back half of the bill upward. The dollar bill is now folded in half, and the face of the bill is upside down (FIG. 40).

Figure 40

Unfold the bill one last time to reveal the face of the bill to your audience (FIG. 41). This simple little trick will occasionally fool an audience. Regardless, kids and adults react to the trick because they've seen it, they know how it works, or they think that they can perform the effect. Using this simple

Figure 41

trick before another money trick allows you to sucker your audience into believing that nothing spectacular is about to happen. *I've found that tactics such as these allow you to nail the audience with mind-blowing magic while their defenses are down.*

Gimmick: A secret device used to perform a magic **effect**.

Glimpse: The action of peeking at a card or item to know its identity (FIG. 42).

Figure 42

Han Ping Chen: The magical transfer of a coin or coins from one hand to the other. This **sleight** is best performed over a flat surface such as a table. *In this explanation, I will describe the transfer of one coin from your left hand to your right hand.* After the coin, such as a half-dollar, is placed openly in your left hand, simply close your left hand into a loose fist. Discreetly, work the coin out of your fist to be held by the tips of the middle and ring fingers of your left hand. The coin should be resting near your left hand's wrist. The audience should see the back of your left hand's fist. From underneath, your left hand should look like the illustration in FIG. 43.

Figure 43

Meanwhile, your right hand should be held open to display its contents. Depending on the **routine**, your right hand could be holding one or several coins. Regardless, your right hand should remain open and held about six inches from your left hand's loose fist (FIG. 44). Your right hand should quickly turn palm down as it attempts to slap the back of your left hand's fist. Before your two hands come into contact, turn your left hand fist up and move it about six inches to your left just after releasing the coin from its grip (FIG. 45).

Figure 44

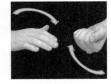
Figure 45

Your right hand should continue moving in a downward motion as it comes into contact with the airborne coin. Keep your right hand moving downward until it stops at the tabletop. The audience will hear coin(s) hit the table, but they should believe there are as many as you held in your right hand a moment ago. This sleight leaves little room for error. Practice this **move** in front of a mirror until you have perfected the swatting action. For further instructions on this sleight, see Bobo's *Modern Coin Magic*.

Haunted Matchbox: A classic **effect** in which a small box of matches mysteriously moves around in the magician's hand.

Hindu Shuffle: This is an excellent means of shuffling for the card worker. It works well not only as a **shuffle**, but also as a **control** and a **force**. Learning this shuffle and the **Overhand Shuffle** will open a window of opportunity to the student of card magic.

Executing the Hindu Shuffle: Hold the pack **face down** near one end with your right hand (FIG. 46). The thumb of your right hand should be on one side and your index finger on **top** of the deck while your middle and ring fingers grip the opposite side. Begin by removing a small **block** of cards from the top of the pack with your left hand's fingertips (FIG. 47). Allow the block of cards to fall into your left hand's palm. Cradle the cards and keep the deck **square** by clutching the pack with the fingers of your left hand (FIG. 48).

Figure 46

Figure 47

Continue to remove small blocks of cards from the top of the deck with your left hand's fingertips. Allow the blocks of cards to fall onto the balance of the deck in your left hand. You are now doing the Hindu Shuffle. Once a small block of cards remains in your right hand, simply toss or place it on top of the balance of the deck in your left hand.

Figure 48

Tips:

♦ *The traditional method of Hindu Shuffling has always seemed a bit choppy to me. I prefer to angle the cards held by my right hand, as shown in FIG. 49. The angle allows the cards to slide onto the balance of the deck in my left hand. The angle of the cards allows them to flow between my left and right hands.*

Figure 49

♦ *Should the blocks of cards in my right hand appear uneven, I simply tilt my left hand toward the floor and allow gravity to straighten them, or I tap the* *pack in my left hand with the cards held by my right hand (FIG. 50). This is a great time to **glimpse** the **face** of the right hand's **packet** to obtain a **force** or **key card**.*

Figure 50

Hindu Shuffle Force: **Shuffle**, or **cut**, or **control**, or place the card to be **forced** on the **face** of the deck (ex: 7 ♦. Execute the **Hindu Shuffle** only this time ask a spectator to call "Stop" at any time to select a card. When the spectator says, "Stop," flash the card on the face of your right hand's **packet** to the audience (FIG. 51). As you turn your head to look away, the audience will see the 7♦ and believe it to be a freely selected card. Place the cards in your right hand on top of those in your

Figure 51

left hand and do with the cards as you wish. Now that you know the identity of the spectator's selection, the deck can be shuffled, and you can divine the card any way you like.

*From now on, when you purchase a card-magic **effect** and it says to use your favorite force, try this one. Several other forces could be used, but none is more diabolical. Practice the Hindu Shuffle and force until you establish a rhythm for handling the cards smoothly without any pauses during the motions. For more information or **routines** using the Hindu Shuffle, see these books:*

Tarbell Course in Magic (Vol. 1) *by Harlan Tarbell*
The Royal Road to Card Magic *by Jean Hugard and Frederick Braue*
Mark Wilson's Complete Course in Magic *by Mark Wilson and Walter Gibson*

Hypnotism: A form of sleep brought on by artificial means, in which there is an unusual suspension of some powers and an unusual activity of others.

Hypnotist: One who performs or practices **hypnotism**.

Illusion: To the average person, an illusion is anything that is deceiving to the eye. The magic profession refers to an illusion as a **stage effect** that uses **apparatus** large enough to hold a human being within it.

Impromptu: **Close-up** magic that is apparently performed off the cuff but is actually well planned out.

Injog: A **jog** held on the side of the deck closest to one's body. *The opposite of an injog is an **outjog*** (FIG. 52).

Figure 52

Invisible Thread: A thread used by magicians that is practically invisible to the eye. Several colors and brands of invisible thread are sold in magic shops. The particular **routine** that requires invisible thread will determine the type of thread you should buy.

Jog: A technique used to make a card protrude slightly from the deck. A jog allows you to keep track of or **control** the card to another place in the deck. *See **injog** and **outjog***.

Kaps' Subtlety: This **sleight-of-hand** technique is used to show both hands empty while actually hiding a coin or coins in one of them. Fred Kaps would **Classic Palm** a coin in his right hand and use the same hand to gesture that the left hand was empty. Being careful to avoid any bad angles, he would run his right hand's thumb down the length of his left hand's palm toward its fingertips (FIG. 53). After this hand-washing motion, he would turn both hands palm down and spread his fingers (FIG. 54). This subtlety creates the illusion of each hand being empty.

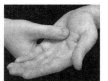
Figure 53

Figure 54

Kelly Bottom Placement: The Kelly Bottom Placement (K.B.P.) is a great method for **controlling** a card to the **bottom** of the deck. When the K.B.P. is done correctly, it is completely undetectable.

Begin by holding the deck in the **Dealer's Grip** with your left hand. **Riffle** or **Dribble** the cards, stopping at the spectator's command. Use your right hand to lift the upper half of the deck where the spectator calls "Stop". Tilt the upper half of the deck toward the audience for all to see the selected card. Stretch your right hand's fingers out straight so as not to obstruct the view of the selected card (FIG. 55).

Figure 55

Ask the spectator to memorize the card they've stopped at. Better yet, have the chosen card initialed with a marker while you hold the **packet**, as shown in FIG. 55. The cards in your left hand should still be held in the **Dealer's Grip**, about waist high, only inches from your body. Extend your right arm toward the audience as you show the selection to all. This should place your right hand's packet above and in front of the cards held by your left hand (FIG. 56).

Figure 56

After showing the chosen card to all, tilt your right hand until the **face** of the packet is perpendicular to the floor. Position your right hand's fingers as shown in FIG. 57. The middle and ring finger of your right hand should press firmly against the underside of the packet. Your right hand's remaining fingers should be used to keep the packet **square**. Remember to hold the cards in your right hand above and in front of the cards held in your left hand.

Figure 57

Lower your right hand and let it approach your left hand to replace the **cut** packet. The tips of the middle and ring fingers of your right hand should exert a slight pressure on the selected card. These fingers should pull the selected card slightly up and over the front edge of the packet. This action will free the selection from the grip of your right thumb and the face of the packet, creating a V-shaped angle between the selection and the face of the packet (FIG. 58). Do not make this angle too wide. This action is masked from the audience by your right hand and the angle at which the cards are held.

Guide the selection onto the **bottom** of the deck as you replace your right hand's packet on top of the cards held by your left hand (FIG. 59). It may be helpful to straighten your left hand's index finger as you ease the selection onto the bottom of your left hand's packet. Act as though your right hand is simply returning the packet and squaring the cards. The audience should be convinced that the selected card is buried within the deck.

Figure 58

Figure 59

The K.B.P. could be repeated with another selection, maintaining both of the "controlled cards" on the face of the deck. The possibilities are endless when you think about it:

◆As the deck is cut, you could **glimpse** the bottom card selection before losing it in the deck.

◆The selection could be **shuffled** or controlled off the bottom of the deck into any specific position you wish.

◆The selection could be **palmed** off the bottom of the deck.

Experiment and come up with your own special use for this multipurpose **sleight**.

The beauty of the K.B.P. is that each movement made with your hands is natural. Although the movements have been broken down for the sake of explanation, remember to execute them with fluidity. The actual **move** should take only a couple of seconds. *For more handling tips and **routine** ideas, see the book* Tarbell Course in Magic (Vol. 3) *by Harlan Tarbell.*

Key Card: A card that is used to help locate the position of another card in a pack of cards.

Layman: A person not belonging to a particular profession, in contrast to those who do. *Laypersons referenced in this book would be non-magicians.*

Loading: The action of placing a concealed item in or under something without the knowledge of the audience.

Load(s): An item or items secretly concealed by the magician that later seem to magically appear in or under something that has been in plain view.

Magician's Choice: A method for **forcing** a particular item on an audience member. The magician preselects an item and manipulates a volunteer to make the same choice. This method of forcing is sometimes referred to as the process of elimination.

Medium: Someone who serves as an intermediary between the living and the dead. Sometimes called a **psychic** or channeler.

Mentalism: The type of **routine** performed by a magician or **mentalist** who executes superhuman feats of the mind.

Mentalist: One who performs **mentalism** or causes things to magically happen using the power of his or her mind.

Mind Reading: **Routines** or **effects** performed by a magician/**mentalist** in which things that are merely thought of are mysteriously divined.

Misdirection: A subtle skill used to hide secret **moves** or **sleights** in magic. There are many ways to divert an audience's attention from the actual workings of an **effect**. For example, a magician's body language or mannerisms, his pattern of speech, his eye contact, a magic wand or even an **assistant** can be used as subterfuge to cause an audience to focus on the magic rather than on the method.

Move: A **sleight** or part of a sleight. *See also **sleight of hand**.*

Muscle Pass: A **sleight** that propels a coin from the magician's hand with great velocity, causing the coin to travel an amazing distance.

Figure 60

The Muscle Pass was popularized by the inventive and award-winning magician John Cornelius. Cornelius teaches the **move** by positioning the coin near the crotch of his thumb (FIG. 60). By squeezing the coin between his muscles at the base of his thumb and below his index and middle finger, the coin is propelled from his hand. Generally, the coin is made to fly upward a couple of feet (FIG. 61).

Figure 61

Needless to say, the Muscle Pass takes much practice. I can honestly say, without a doubt, it is the most difficult coin maneuver that I have ever learned. The practice was well worth it, though. When I perform the Muscle Pass, it always gets a jaw-drop reaction from the audience.

*When I sought to learn this amazing sleight, there were no books or videos on the market that showed Cornelius' clever handling. Thus, like many magicians, I taught myself how to do the move. I believed that the Muscle Pass was supposed to be executed from the **Classic Palm** position (FIG. 62). I practiced and practiced until the coin would jump a short distance. Several calluses later, the coin finally would pop out of my hand a foot or more, just like real magic.*

Figure 62

What kind of coin should you use? I prefer to use half- dollars because:
◆ *Most coin magic is performed with half-dollars. Work with what you are accustomed to, though.*
◆ *The edge of a half-dollar is milled. The milled edge makes the coin pop from your hand more easily when doing the move. I've tried using a coin such as an English penny (without milled edges), and it tends to cut into my hand during the squeezing action required by the Muscle Pass.*

◆*Half-dollars are the correct size and weight to accomplish the Muscle Pass. Your hand appears cramped when attempting the Muscle Pass with a coin smaller than a half-dollar, such as a quarter. Silver dollars are too big to use in executing this maneuver convincingly, and their weight makes them more difficult to propel from your hand.*

The magic of the Muscle Pass is that the hand performing the sleight, usually the right, appears absolutely still during the moment of execution. Do not make the mistake of unconsciously bouncing your right hand upward to help the coin fly, or you will spoil the **effect**. Use only the muscles in your hand to make the magic happen. Finally, remember to use some **misdirection** to take attention off the hand executing the sleight. *For Mr. Cornelius' original handling and **routine** ideas, buy, borrow or steal the video:* Classic Renditions (Vol. I) *by L&L Publishing.*

Needle Thru Balloon: An **effect** sold in magic shops in which a large needle penetrates a full-blown nine-inch clear balloon.

Novelty Store: A store that sells **gag** gifts, practical jokes and sometimes magic **apparatus**.

One-Handed Cut: The action of **cutting** a pack of cards and completing the cut with the use of one hand. *For an example, see the **Charlier Pass** (FIG. 63).*

Figure 63

One-Handed Shuffle: The action of **shuffling** a pack of cards with one hand (FIG. 64). *Rather than explaining this difficult **sleight-of-hand** maneuver, I recommend going straight to the source. The best source in print is* Dai Vernon's More Inner Secrets of Card Magic *by Lewis Ganson.*

Figure 64

Opener: An effect or routine used to begin a magic act and grab the audience's attention.

Outjog: A **jog** held on the side of the deck away from one's body. *The opposite of an outjog is an **injog** (FIG. 65).*

Figure 65

Overhand Shuffle: This is an easy **shuffle** and an effective means of **controlling** cards. Begin by holding the pack lengthwise in your left hand.

Hold the short edges of the pack with your right fingers and thumb. Press on the **top** of the pack with your left thumb. With your right hand, draw a large **block** of cards from the back of the pack.

Place the cards in your right hand on top of those in your left hand. With your left hand's thumb, pull a few cards off the block in your right hand onto the **packet** in your left hand (FIG. 66). Repeat this action several times until all of the cards in your right hand have been distributed on top of the cards in your left hand. Practice this shuffle until you can do it with your eyes closed. *For more tips or* **effects** *with the Overhand Shuffle, see* The Royal Road to Card Magic *by Jean Hugard and Frederick Braue.*

Figure 66

Packet (of cards): A small quantity of cards that are usually held **squared** together.

Palming: The action of hiding an item (such as a ball, coin or card) in the hand. A hand that palms an item should try to appear as natural as possible. The hand that palms an item is sometimes referred to as the *guilty* or *dirty* hand.

Patter: Rehearsed lines or stories that a magician uses to accompany his **effects** or **tricks**. Patter is one of the elements of **misdirection**.

Penetration: The magical passing of one solid object through another.

Poker Size Cards: Playing cards that are 3$\frac{1}{2}$ inches long and 2$\frac{1}{2}$ inches wide (FIG. 67).

Prearranged Deck: *See* **Stacked Deck**.

Figure 67

Prediction: The act of telling the future; also, that which is foretold.

Production: An **effect** in which items are produced from the magician's bare hands or an empty receptacle. *See also* **loads**.

Psychic: An event pertaining to forces or mental processes outside the possibilities defined by natural or scientific laws. A person who is sensitive to things beyond the natural range of perception.

Retention of Vision Vanish: A **sleight** used to make small objects visibly disappear from the magician's hand.

Method: *Let's assume that you wish to make a half-dollar vanish.* Pick up the half-dollar with your right hand, pinching it between the index finger and thumb. Place the half-dollar into the center of the open palm of your left hand (FIG. 68). Do not release the half-dollar from its pinched-grip by your right hand.

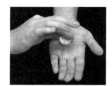
Figure 68

Before proceeding, keep the fingers of your right hand stretched upward. This position allows your audience never to lose sight of the half-dollar. Now close your left hand's fingers until they meet the coin (FIG. 69). Maintain a loose grip around the half-dollar with your left hand.

Figure 69

Relax the second, third and fourth fingers of your right hand so they touch the fingers of your left hand's loose fist (FIG. 70). Do not release the half-dollar from its pinched grip by your right hand. When performing each of these movements, try not to appear robotic in your actions.

Figure 70

Prepare to remove the coin from your left hand. Do not pull the coin out from the back of your left hand. Rather, separate your hands, moving your left hand to your left and your right hand to your right (FIG. 71). *Afterward, in most scenarios, I prefer to let my right arm relax at my side with the concealed object in the* **Finger Rest** *position.* Keep eye contact with your own left hand, directing the audience's attention there. *Usually, I pretend to fidget with the imaginary object concealed in my left hand by wiggling its fingers slightly; this subtlety was shown to me by Dallas' Johnny Brown.*

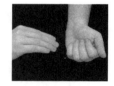
Figure 71

Apparently you are now holding an object in your closed left fist. You can go to your pocket with your right hand to fetch some "magic dust" while ditching the object. You could **load** the object into or under something. Do not simply open your left hand to show that the object has vanished. Logically, the audience will think that the missing object is in your right hand. Show that the object has vanished when you can prove your right hand is empty, or when you are able to produce it from somewhere else.

To comprehend the Retention of Vision Vanish, I have taken the time to try to break up each of the movements necessary to execute the sleight. However, your movements should not appear to be broken. Your hands and fingers should move with fluidity. If you hesitate at any moment, your actions will cause the audience to be suspicious. "The Professor," Dai Vernon, said it best: In the audience's mind, "Suspicion is the method". For other coin vanishes and coin sleights, see these books:

Modern Coin Magic *by J. B. Bobo*
Expert Coin Magic *by David Roth*

Reversed Card Force: A means of **forcing** a card in which the magician apparently never touches the deck.

Start by removing the card you wish to force. Turn your **force card face up** and place it about six to eight cards from the **bottom** of the deck. **Square** the cards and place them into their cardbox. You are now ready to use the Reversed Card Force.

During the performance, remove the cards from their box. Execute a couple of **false shuffles** and/or **false cuts**. While supposedly mixing the cards, carelessly flash the **faces** of the cards to suggest they are ordinary. Do not expose your reversed force card. Hand the pack to a spectator and instruct your helper to place the cards under the table so no one can see them.

Explain to the spectator that he or she should spread through the cards and select one but not look at it just yet. After choosing a card, tell the spectator to place the selection face up on **top** of the deck. Tell the spectator to **cut** the pack and complete the cut. This will bury the card in the deck with the face-up force card about six to eight cards above it.

Tell the spectator to look into his or her lap, spread the cards and memorize the first face-up card that he or she comes to. Once the spectator has looked at the force card, have him or her place the cards back into their box. It's usually a good idea to have the spectator write down the name of the selection so it will not be forgotten. You can now reveal the card in a mystical manner.

There are many other forces that you could use; a few of them can be found in this glossary. However, this force is unique, since it requires no **sleight of hand**. In addition, all of the action takes place in the spectator's hands. *Other great forces can be found in the booklet* 202 Methods of Forcing *by Theodore Annemann.*

Ribbon Spreading: A **flourish** used to display the cards in a spread-out fashion. Begin by placing a pack of cards onto a smooth surface such as a tabletop. Most magicians find the Ribbon Spread easiest to do with a good-quality pack of cards on a cloth surface. Surfaces like glass tabletops are more difficult to work on.

Make sure the pack is **squared**. Grasp the deck of cards from above with your right hand. Your right hand's thumb should be at the center of the back of the deck. The middle and ring fingers of your right hand should be stretched over the front center of the deck. Your right hand's index finger should lie naturally across the left side of the deck while you are gripping it.

Now with a slight downward pressure from your right hand's index finger, move your right hand and arm to your right. The cards should begin to spread apart evenly off the **bottom** of the deck. Continue sliding the balance of the deck along the table's surface. The position of your right hand's fingers is used as a guide to keep the cards evenly spread (FIG. 72).

Figure 72

As with all other **sleights**, practice makes perfect. Practice this technique over and over until it becomes second nature to you. The Ribbon Spread is one of the easiest and most practical sleights a card magician can learn. It's a great way to offer a card to a spectator or to show off some of your hard work as a magician. *For further instructions on this useful flourish, see these sources:*

Now You See It, Now You Don't *by Bill Tarr*
Mark Wilson's Complete Course in Magic *by Mark Wilson and Walter Gibson*

Riffle False Shuffle: A **false shuffle** used to convince an audience that a pack of cards has been thoroughly mixed. Pick up the top half of a **squared** deck of cards off the table with your right hand. We will call this half of the deck block A. Your right hand's thumb should grip one end of block A while your right hand's other fingers grip the opposite end of the **block**.

166

Pick up the other half of the deck with your left hand. We will call this half of the deck block B. Your left hand should grip block B just as your right hand is gripping block A. Your thumbs should be positioned naturally and close to your body. The grip used by both hands is the same as during a **dovetail shuffle**.

Place the blocks against the tabletop or against your body and begin **riffling** the inner corners of the blocks together. The interlaced halves of the deck should appear to be in a V-formation (FIG. 73). Be sure that the uppermost card on top of block A remains the uppermost card after the shuffling action is complete. At this point during the shuffle, the cards have actually been mixed.

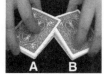

Figure 73

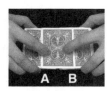

Figure 74

Push the **top** card off block A half of the way onto block B, with your right hand's index finger, to hide the next action. Pivot the cards in your left hand to your left and the cards in your right hand to your right (FIG. 74). This action should separate the interlaced halves from one another. The uppermost card should mask the separate halves of the deck.

Act as if you are completing the shuffle while you are actually lifting block A on top of block B. Pretend that you have shuffled the cards, and square them as you normally would. This false shuffle should look and sound like a standard shuffle. *Typically, I'll perform this shuffle before a card **routine** two or three times, as necessary.*

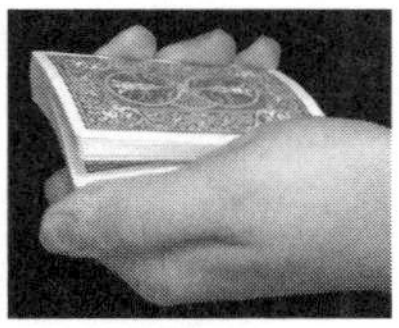

Riffling: The action and noise created when a magician runs his thumb down the corner of a pack of cards (FIG. 75).

Figure 75

Routine: A sequence of **tricks** or **effects** that blend. A series of routines is usually called an act.

Seance: A meeting of people to receive spirit communication from beyond. During a seance people usually sit around a table with hands joined. The leader or head of the seance is referred to as a **medium**.

Set-up: The preparation of a magic **routine** unseen by the audience. Measures taken before a performance to assure an **effect's** successful outcome.

Shell Coin: A hollow coin that appears ordinary on one side.

Short Card: A playing card cut a little shorter than the other cards in the deck (FIG. 76). Placing a short card in a deck allows the magician to locate it easily by **riffling** the ends of a **squared** deck of cards.

Shuffle: The process of mixing a deck of cards.

Si Stebbins System: A **prearranged deck** that allows you to know the identity of any card selected. The cards are stacked by suit and by number. See the following order. . . .

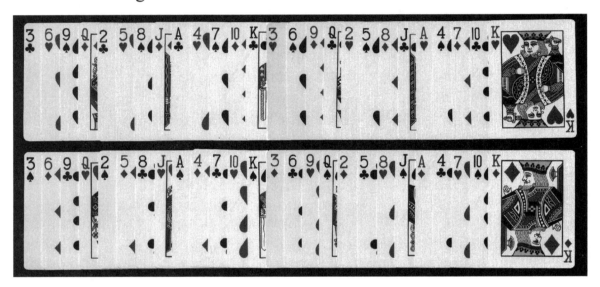

Each card in the sequence has a value of three more than the preceding card. So if the **top** card is a Two, the next card is a Five, the next an Eight, etc. The suit order of the system is Clubs, Hearts, Spades, and Diamonds. This arrangement of the suits is better known as the "CHaSeD" order. In the "CHaSeD" order, if the top card were the Ace of Clubs, the next card would be the Four of Hearts, followed by the Seven of Spades. Or if the top card were the Ten of Hearts, the next card would be the King of Spades, followed by the Three of Diamonds, etc.

The **face cards** have numerical values as well. Jacks are equal to eleven. Queens are equal to twelve. Kings are equal to thirteen. The Jokers are not used. So if the top card is a Ten, the next card would be a King (10 + 3 = 13). After the King, the numerical order starts over with an Ace. *Study the card layout provided above.*

<u>Routine</u>: Spread the cards from hand to hand **face down** and ask someone to touch a card. Once the card has been selected, **outjog** it. Separating the deck at the outjogged card, hand the spectator the selected card (FIG. 77). With a stack of face-down cards in each hand, place the cards in your left hand on top of those in your right. You have just **cut** the deck. *The act of cutting the pack should go unnoticed by the audience.*

Figure 77

Glimpse at the card on the **face** of the deck as you **square** the cards. Knowing the value of the **bottom** card, add three, and the next suit in the "CHaSeD" order, to identify the selected card. After revealing the card in a magical manner, have the card returned to the face or top of the deck to maintain the system's order. *The beauty of the Si Stebbins System is that the deck may be cut as many times as you like without disturbing the cards' order.*

*There are other prearranged card systems. However, none is as simple to use as the Si Stebbins System. The only flaw with this system is that the cards are in a perfect red-black-red-black order. The system was never meant to be **ribbon spread face up** for an audience to examine. If you feel you must show the faces of the cards, simply spread them face up in small clumps from hand to hand (FIG. 78).*

Figure 78

*I have been using the Si Stebbins System since I was six years old. This system transformed a boy into a **mind reader**. As a child, I knew the system was a powerful tool to employ. Even today, I realize the ability the system has to amaze audiences, and I quote from Julien J. Proskauer's (1934) book* How'd Ja Do That?:

"There is just as much pride of achievement in fooling an audience with a Si Stebbins pack which requires little practice to use successfully, as there is in amazing them with some trick based on a side-steal, pass, back-palm, bottom-deal, or any other sleight which may require years of practice to perfect."

Sleeving: The secret act of hiding an item in one's sleeve (FIG. 79). Sleeving is used during a magic **routine** to **vanish** or sometimes **produce** objects. *One magician of our day, Rocco Silano, has taken the art of sleeving to its highest level. For more information about his techniques and routines, read*

Figure 79

Sleight: A secret movement of the hands used in magic. *Referred to simply as a **move** by some magicians.*

Sleight of Hand: The name for secret **moves** in magic. **Sleights** are necessary to make some **tricks** work. Typically, acting and talking complement sleight of hand, making it easier to perform more discreetly.

Slop Shuffle: This **false shuffle** creates the illusion of **face-up** cards being mixed with **face-down** cards.

Before starting, **spring the cards** or squeeze them lengthwise, putting a slight bow in the deck (FIG. 80). Hold the deck in the **Dealer's Grip**, face down, in your left hand. With your left hand's thumb, push a few cards off the **top** of the deck into your right hand. As you take away the small **packet** of cards with your right hand, thumb off a few more cards with the left hand.

Figure 80

Place the cards in your right hand face up on top of the thumbed-off cards in your left hand. As you do this, lift up the thumbed-off group of cards. You should now have a small packet of face-up cards on top of a small packet of face-down cards in your right hand (FIG. 81). Thumb off a few more cards from the deck with your left hand. Reverse the cards in your right hand and place them on top of the thumbed-off cards in your left hand.

Figure 81

Lift the thumbed-off **block** of cards again. Continue to reverse the cards in your right hand on top of the thumbed-off cards in your left hand. Repeat these actions swiftly until you've gone through the entire deck. Once you're done, hold the deck **square** in the Dealer's Grip with your left hand.

Your audience should be convinced that you have randomly mixed face-up cards with face-down cards. Actually, the top half of the deck is face up and the bottom half is face down. There is a natural break between these two halves, since you put a slight bow in the deck before you began. Do not spread the cards at this point, or you will spoil the illusion.

You will now begin the sequence to right all of the cards so they are face down. Begin by cutting one-fourth of the deck away with your right hand as you say, "Cards are face up". Place the cards in your right hand back on top of the cards in your left hand. Use your right hand to separate the halves of the deck at its natural break, near the middle of the pack. As you remove the top half of the deck with your right hand, look at the cards in your left hand and say, "Cards are face down."

Slyly, turn over the cards in your right hand as you comment, "Cards are back to back." Place the reversed block of cards face down in your right hand on top of those in your left hand. Pretend to do something mysterious by shaking the deck or **riffling** one of the deck's corners. **Fan** or **ribbon spread** the cards to reveal that all of the cards are facing the same direction.

This simple false shuffle receives great reactions from laymen. *Originally this false shuffle was called the "S.L. Reversed Card," when published by Sid Lorraine. This shuffle appeared in the 1937 book* Subtle Problems You Will Do, *written by John Braun and Stewart Judah. Another reference I found for the Slop Shuffle was in* Royal Road to Card Magic *by Jean Hugard and Frederick Braue. On page 195 of* Royal Road *is an **effect** called "A Tipsy Trick," which gives the reader various tips on the Slop Shuffle and a great **routine**.*

Spellbound: An **effect** devised by late great Dai Vernon in which an American half-dollar magically **changes** to an English penny time and again. *For more information about this **routine**, see the book* Stars of Magic, *published by D. Robbins.*

Spot Card: A number card *(ex: Ace through Ten)*.

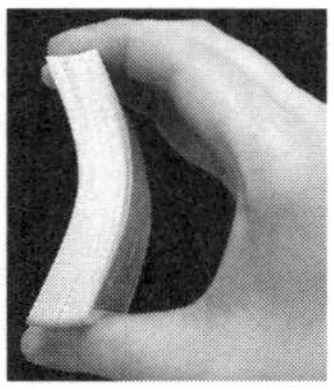

Figure 82

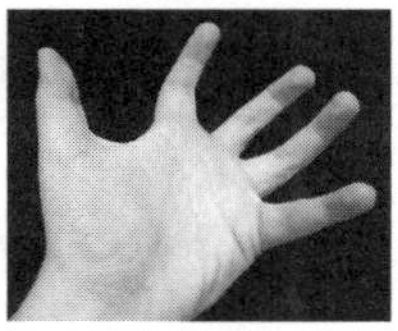

Springing Cards: A **sleight** that makes cards magically leap a surprising distance from one of the magician's hands to the other.

Figure 83

Method: Hold the pack lengthwise in your right hand, squeezing the pack as shown in FIG. 82. Position your left hand with its fingers outstretched, ready to catch the springing cards (FIG. 83). Continue to squeeze the pack until cards begin leaping from the **face** of the pack (FIG. 84).

Figure 84

Your hands should be a few inches apart as you begin. As the cards start springing, pull your hands farther apart. The distance that you should pull your hands apart depends on how far you can spring the cards in a straight direction. Practice the springing action and perfect the act of catching the cards.

Once the majority of the cards have landed in your left hand, bring your hands together. Place the remaining cards in your right hand on top of those in your left hand. **Square** the pack, and you are ready for your next card miracle.

*Springing cards is fun to do and fun for your audience to watch. As you squeeze the pack, it puts a slight bow in the deck. I have found that "bowing the deck" helps to **fan** cards and execute other common card sleights. Whenever I open a new pack of cards, I like to spring the deck **face up** and **face down** a few times. Springing the deck helps to break the pack in. For further instructions on this useful sleight, see these books:*

Now You See It, Now You Don't *by Bill Tarr*
Mark Wilson's Complete Course in Magic *by Mark Wilson and Walter Gibson*

Squaring Cards: The act of straightening all of the cards in a pack until they are aligned or even (FIG. 85).

Figure 85

Stacked Deck: A card or cards put into an order to achieve some means or accomplish a **trick**. *Also known as a **Prearranged Deck**.*

Stage: The kind of magic one usually sees on a large stage. Most stage magicians perform **illusions** with the help of an assistant. Stage magic is known for large **effects** accompanied by music, large animals, spectacular theatrics, and special effects.

Stand-up: The kind of magic one normally sees on a small stage or in small venues. Typically, stand-up **routines** are performed by individuals who call on volunteers for help. Stand-up magicians use simple props that are visible to a large audience. *Also referred to as cabaret magic.*

Strolling: The type of magic performed for people who are in small groups, whether they are sitting or standing. The magician who strolls through a crowd usually performs **close-up**, **mentalism** or comical **routines**. *Also*

Swing False Cut: This is a **false cut** that creates the illusion of cards actually being **cut**, thus keeping the cards in exactly the same order. Grasp the **face-down** deck of cards from above with your right hand. Your right hand's thumb should be at the back right corner of the deck. Your right hand's ring fingertip should be on the front right corner of the deck. Your right hand's middle fingertip should rest against your ring finger (FIG. 86)

Figure 86

Place your right hand's index finger over the front left corner of the deck. Use the right hand's index finger to pivot the top half of the deck to your left. This is the *swing* in the swing false cut. Here is a bottom view of what your right hand and the cards should look like (FIG. 87).

Figure 87

The top half of the deck should be taken with your left hand. The cards in your right hand should be brought from under the table and then up and over the back of the cards in your left hand and placed on the table. Use your right hand to place the cards in your left hand on top of the cards on the table. This illusion, when done properly, should convince your audience that the deck was cut. *For other false cutting techniques see* Royal Road to Card Magic *by Jean Hugard and Frederick Braue.*

Switch: A **sleight** used to secretly substitute one object for another.

Table-Hopping: *See **strolling**.*

Tarot Cards: A special pack of cards designed to foretell the future and give insight into one's life (FIG. 88). Today's modern playing cards are descendants of the medieval tarot.

Figure 88

Thumb Palm: A concealment used to hold a coin or other small objects. Simply clip the object within the crotch of your thumb to hide it in the hand (FIG. 89). The audience should see only the back of the guilty hand, as with most coin palms.

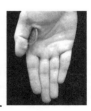

Figure 89

Trick: An **effect** or **routine** that is made to fool and entertain an audience.

Top (of the Deck): The uppermost card or portion of the deck (FIG. 90).

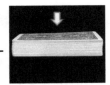

Figure 90

Vanish: The act of making an object disappear from sight.

Walk-Around: *See strolling*.

Walking a Coin: A **flourish** used to make a coin walk across the knuckles of the magician's hand.

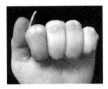

Figure 91

All of the actions below are done with one hand made into a fist. Choose the hand that works best for you. Hold a large coin, such as a half-dollar, against your first finger with your thumb (FIG. 91). Tip the coin onto the back of your first finger with your thumb. Grip the coin between your first and second fingers with your second finger (FIG. 92).

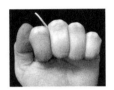

Figure 92

Tilt the coin onto the back of your second finger with your first finger. Roll the coin over onto your third finger, using your second finger. Tip the coin into the gap between your third and little fingers. Your thumb should cross under your little finger to catch the coin as it slides between your third and little fingers into your hand (FIG. 93).

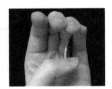

Figure 93

Typically the magician slides the coin from under his fingers back onto the top of his hand to repeat the walking action. *Once the coin gets to the last joint, between the third and little fingers, I prefer to reverse the previous actions, walking the coin backward. I call this moon-walking a coin.* Walking the coin backward is no more difficult than walking it forward, but audiences seem to be more impressed with moon-walking.

Wise Guy: *An individual who uses **cons** or **bar bets** to try to make others look stupid or to win something of monetary value.*

Zombie Ball: A **routine** performed by **stage** magicians in which a large metal ball floats mysteriously in the air.

ABOUT THE AUTHOR

Diamond Jim Tyler was born in 1970. By 1972 he knew every card in a pack of cards. His grandmother Pauline would give him playing cards when he was a baby each time she saw him. This is how Jim learned to count and became adept at handling cards. Little did his grandmother know that she was providing him with the tools of his future trade, which would ultimately launch his career and take him around the world.

In 1976, Jim's parents took him to the *Magic Kingdom,* better known as Disney World in Florida. There he purchased his first magic book entitled *Magic with Cards* by Garcia and Schindler from the Disney magic shop. Within in a year Jim mastered all 113 tricks in the book. That book transformed a boy who was fascinated with cards into a boy who could fascinate others with cards.

In 1985, Jim discovered a magic shop in Garland, TX called *Positively Magic.* By 1986 Jim had purchased and learned almost every trick in the shop so the owner offered him a job there. Jim jumped at the chance specifically so he could receive the employee discount. That same year Jim began performing his magic professionally by working tableside in restaurants and began inventing his own effects.

Shortly after this, Jim became known as *Diamond Jim* and worked his way through college performing magic. During these college years Jim began compiling this book, which was originally titled *Pockets Full of Miracles: Secrets from the Repertoire of a Professional Close-Up Magician.* That book was later released on DVD and has sold in the thousands.

From there Diamond Jim has gone on to market dozens of other effects (like the *Diamond Deck),* other DVDs (like *DiaMonte*) and author more books like *Bamboozlers: The Book of Bankable Bar Betchas, Brain Bogglers, Belly Busters and Bewitchery.* He has also received awards from the *Texas Association of Magicians* and the *International Brotherhood of Magicians.*

Since 1986 he has been one of the top magicians in the Dallas / Fort Worth area and has built an impressive resume. Some of his career highlights have been working at the *Magic Castle* in Hollywood, the *Magic Circle* in London, the *Improv Comedy Club,* performing on TV, acting as a consultant for the motion picture *Mirrors,* starring Kiefer Sutherland, and performing as a headliner at the world's largest magic convention in history, which took place in Blackpool, England, in February of 2010.

Nowadays, Diamond Jim travels the world sharing his effects through his lectures for magicians. To date he has performed in half of the states in the U.S. plus nineteen other countries. His personal goal is to perform in all 50 U.S. states and to visit as many countries as he can. Diamond Jim resides just north of Dallas, with his wife Kathy and their pet iguana. To learn more about Diamond Jim and his magic, visit www.djtyler.com.

DOVER BOOKS ON MAGIC

101 EASY-TO-DO MAGIC TRICKS, Bill Tarr. (0-486-27367-9)

ABBOTT'S ENCYCLOPEDIA OF ROPE TRICKS FOR MAGICIANS, Stewart James. (0-486-23206-9)

THE ART OF MAGIC, T. Nelson Downs. (0-486-24005-3)

A BOOK OF MAGIC FOR YOUNG MAGICIANS: THE SECRETS OF ALKAZAR, Allan Zola Kronzek. (0-486-27134-X)

CARD CONTROL: PRACTICAL METHODS AND FORTY ORIGINAL CARD EXPERIMENTS, Arthur H. Buckley. (0-486-27757-7)

CARD MAGIC FOR AMATEURS AND PROFESSIONALS, Bill Simon. (0-486-40188-X)

CARD MANIPULATIONS, Jean Hugard. (0-486-20539-8)

CARD TRICKS FOR BEGINNERS, Wilfrid Jonson. (0-486-43465-6)

CLASSIC CARD TRICKS, Edward Victor. (0-486-43355-2)

EASY MAGIC TRICKS, Joseph Leeming. (0-486-45555-6)

EASY-TO-DO MAGIC TRICKS FOR CHILDREN, Karl Fulves. (0-486-27613-9)

EASY-TO-MASTER MENTAL MAGIC, James L. Clark. (0-486-47954-4)

ELLIS STANYON'S BEST CARD TRICKS, Karl Fulves. (0-486-40530-3)

ENCYCLOPEDIA OF CARD TRICKS, Jean Hugard. (0-486-21252-1)

THE EXPERT AT THE CARD TABLE: THE CLASSIC TREATISE ON CARD MANIPULATION, S. W. Erdnase. (0-486-28597-9)

EXPERT CARD TECHNIQUE, Hugard/Braué. (0-486-21755-8)

FOOLPROOF CARD TRICKS FOR THE AMATEUR MAGICIAN, Karl Fulves. (0-486-47270-1)

HOUDINI ON MAGIC, Harry Houdini. (0-486-20384-0)

MAGIC AND SHOWMANSHIP: A HANDBOOK FOR CONJURERS, Henning Nelms. (0-486-41087-0)

MAGIC FOR EVERYBODY, Joseph Leeming. (0-486-46146-7)

MAGICIAN'S MAGIC, Paul Curry. (0-486-43176-2)

MARTIN GARDNER'S TABLE MAGIC, Martin Gardner. (0-486-40403-X)

MASKELYNE'S BOOK OF MAGIC, Jasper Maskelyne. (0-486-47177-2)

MASTER MAGIC: ASTOUNDING MAGIC TRICKS THAT YOU CAN DO IN A FLASH, Dover. (0-486-44065-6)

MATHEMAGIC: MAGIC, PUZZLES AND GAMES WITH NUMBERS, Royal V. Heath. (0-486-20110-4)

MATHEMATICS, MAGIC AND MYSTERY, Martin Gardner. (0-486-20335-2)

MENTAL MAGIC: SUREFIRE TRICKS TO AMAZE YOUR FRIENDS, Martin Gardner. (0-486-47495-X)

MODERN COIN MAGIC, J. B. Bobo. (0-486-24258-7)

MY BEST SELF-WORKING CARD TRICKS, Karl Fulves. (0-486-41981-9)

PRACTICAL MENTAL MAGIC, Theodore Annemann. (0-486-24426-1)

PRESTO! MAGIC FOR THE BEGINNER, George Schindler. (0-486-47759-2)

PROFESSIONAL MAGIC FOR AMATEURS, Walter B. Gibson. (0-486-23012-0)

THE ROYAL ROAD TO CARD MAGIC, Hugard/Braué. (0-486-40843-4)

SCARNE ON CARD TRICKS, John Scarne. (0-486-42735-8)

SCARNE'S MAGIC TRICKS, John Scarne. (0-486-42779-X)

SCIENCE MAGIC TRICKS, Nathan Shalit. (0-486-40042-5)

THE SECRETS OF HOUDINI, J. C. Cannell. (0-486-22913-0)

SELF-WORKING CARD TRICKS, Karl Fulves. 90-486-23334-0)

SELF-WORKING CLOSE-UP CARD MAGIC, Karl Fulves. (0-486-28124-8)

SELF-WORKING COIN MAGIC, Karl Fulves. (0-486-26179-4)

SELF-WORKING HANDKERCHIEF MAGIC, Karl Fulves. (0-486-25694-4)

SELF-WORKING MENTAL MAGIC, Karl Fulves. (0-486-23806-7)

SELF-WORKING NUMBER MAGIC, Karl Fulves. (0-486-24391-5)